Cambridge Elements

Elements in Evolutionary Economics
edited by
John Foster
University of Queensland
Jason Potts
RMIT University
Isabel Almudi
University of Zaragoza
Francisco Fatas-Villafranca
University of Zaragoza
David A. Harper
New York University

EVOLUTIONARY GAMES AND THE REPLICATOR DYNAMICS

Saul Mendoza-Palacios
Center for Research and Teaching in Economics (CIDE)

Onésimo Hernández-Lerma
Center for Research and Advanced Studies of the National Polytechnic Institute (CINVESTAV-IPN)

CAMBRIDGE
UNIVERSITY PRESS

CAMBRIDGE
UNIVERSITY PRESS

Shaftesbury Road, Cambridge CB2 8EA, United Kingdom

One Liberty Plaza, 20th Floor, New York, NY 10006, USA

477 Williamstown Road, Port Melbourne, VIC 3207, Australia

314–321, 3rd Floor, Plot 3, Splendor Forum, Jasola District Centre,
New Delhi – 110025, India

103 Penang Road, #05–06/07, Visioncrest Commercial, Singapore 238467

Cambridge University Press is part of Cambridge University Press & Assessment,
a department of the University of Cambridge.

We share the University's mission to contribute to society through the pursuit of education, learning and research at the highest international levels of excellence.

www.cambridge.org
Information on this title: www.cambridge.org/9781009472302

DOI: 10.1017/9781009472319

When citing this work, please include a reference to the DOI 10.1017/9781009472319

First published 2024

A catalogue record for this publication is available from the British Library.

ISBN 978-1-009-47230-2 Hardback
ISBN 978-1-009-47232-6 Paperback
ISSN 2514-3573 (online)
ISSN 2514-3581 (print)

Additional resources for this publication at www.cambridge.org/evolutionary-games

Evolutionary Games and the Replicator Dynamics

Elements in Evolutionary Economics

DOI: 10.1017/9781009472319
First published online: May 2024

Saul Mendoza-Palacios
Center for Research and Teaching in Economics (CIDE)

Onésimo Hernández-Lerma
Center for Research and Advanced Studies of the National Polytechnic Institute (CINVESTAV-IPN)

Author for correspondence: Saul Mendoza-Palacios, saul.mendoza@cide.edu

Abstract: This Element introduces the replicator dynamics for symmetric and asymmetric games where the strategy sets are metric spaces. Under this hypothesis the replicator dynamics evolves in a Banach space of finite signed measures. The authors provide a general framework to study the stability of the replicator dynamics for evolutionary games in this Banach space. This allows them to establish a relation between Nash equilibria and the stability of the replicator for normal-form games applicable to oligopoly models, theory of international trade, public good models, the tragedy of commons, and the war of attrition game among others. They also provide conditions to approximate the replicator dynamics on a space of measures by means of a finite-dimensional dynamical system and a sequence of measure-valued Markov processes.

Keywords: games with continuous strategy spaces, asymmetric evolutionary games, evolutionary games, population games, replicator dynamics

JEL classifications: C72, C73, E14, O25

ISBNs: 9781009472302 (HB), 9781009472326 (PB), 9781009472319 (OC)
ISSNs: 2514-3573 (online), 2514-3581 (print)

Contents

1 Introduction and Technical Preliminaries 1

2 Normal-Form Games 10

3 Evolutionary Games: The Asymmetric Case 17

4 Evolutionary Games: Symmetric Case 37

5 Finite-Dimensional Approximations 52

6 The Replicator Dynamics as a Deterministic Approximation 67

7 Conclusions and Suggestions for Future Research 77

List of Symbols and Abbreviations 81

References 83

An Online Appendix is available at
www.cambridge.org/evolutionary-games

1 Introduction and Technical Preliminaries

1.1 Introduction

Evolutionary games form a class of noncooperative games in which the interaction of strategies is studied using evolutionary ideas from two different approaches, static and dynamic. The static approach captures evolutionary concepts through defining and studying equilibrium terms. The dynamic approach, on the other hand, studies the interaction of strategies as a dynamical process determined by a system of differential equations. This Element concerns the dynamic approach with a specific dynamical system known as the replicator dynamics. We are particularly interested in the stability of the replicator dynamics for evolutionary games in which the strategy set is a measurable set or, more precisely, a separable metric space.

An evolutionary game is said to be *symmetric* if there are two players only and, furthermore, they have the same strategy sets and the same payoff functions. This type of game models interactions of strategies of a single population and forms part of the so-called population games. On the other hand, *asymmetric* evolutionary games, also known as *multipopulation* games, are those in which there is a finite set of players (or populations), each of which has a different set of strategies and different payoff functions.

Game models with strategies in general measurable spaces are important because they include essentially all the models that appear in theory and applications, from games with finite strategy sets to games with strategies in metric spaces such as some models in oligopoly theory, international trade theory, war of attrition, and public goods, among others. With our proposed model we can introduce evolutionary dynamics in games where the strategy set is a Borel space (that is, a Borel subset of a complete and separable metric space). We have, consequently, that the dynamical system lives in a Banach space, which in our case is a space of finite signed measures. In particular, if the strategy set is finite, then the dynamical system is in $\mathbb{R}^m$, where m is the number of strategies of a player for symmetric games, or the total number of strategies of all players for asymmetric games.

The main objective of this Element is to present a general, unified framework to study the existence of solutions and the stability of the replicator dynamics for games with metric strategy sets. This means that, first, we establish conditions for the existence of solutions to the replicator dynamics for asymmetric games, and also conditions that ensure the stability of the system in this asymmetric case. Bomze and Pötscher (1989) suggest an approach (similar to that in Selten (1980) for the case with finite strategy sets) in which asymmetric games are reduced to the symmetric case; for details, see Section 3.2. This approach, however, has some disadvantages. For instance, the relationship between Nash equilibria and the replicator dynamics is unclear. It is also unclear how to extend stability concepts and results to the asymmetric case. In contrast, with our proposed model it is easy to see the relationship between a Nash equilibrium and the replicator dynamics (see Section 3.4) and, in addition, stability concepts have a natural extension from the symmetric case to the asymmetric situation (see Section 3.5).

Second, for symmetric games we study stability criteria in a fairly general context, with respect to different topologies and metrics on a space of measures. We can thus, for instance, relate the Nash equilibria of a certain normal-form game with the stability of the replicator dynamics under different metrics (see Section 4.4), and similarly for strongly uninvadable strategies (Section 4.3), a refinement of Nash equilibria.

Third, we can obtain quite general, and at the same time precise results on the approximation of the replicator dynamics by different approximating models, which include finite-dimensional dynamic systems. These approximations can be in a strong form, using the variational norm (Section 5.2), or in a weak form, using the Kantorovich–Rubinstein norm (Section 5.3).

Fourth, we study the replicator dynamics as a limit of a sequence of Markov processes (see Section 6), where each Markov process describes a stochastic interaction among the characteristics (genotypes or actions) of the individuals. This stochastic interaction can be studied by means of a determinist dynamic under some hypotheses.

Concerning some related literature, conditions for the existence of solutions to the replicator dynamics in measure spaces in the symmetric case are given by several authors, including Bomze (1991), Oechssler and Riedel (2001), and more generally (including dynamics different from the replicator equation) by Cleveland and Ackleh (2013). In Section 3.3 we present conditions for the existence of solutions to the replicator dynamics in measure spaces in the asymmetric case and some other important results.

Similarly, conditions for stability have been developed with respect to different topologies, as in, for instance, Bomze (1990), Oechssler and Riedel (2001, 2002), Eshel and Sansone (2003), Van Veelen and Spreij (2009), and Cressman and Hofbauer (2005). In Section 3.5, we present stability results for the replicator dynamics in the asymmetric case. In Section 4.3, we present a brief review of stability results in the symmetric case. Also in Section 4.3 we establish a result that characterizes the stability of the replicator dynamics with respect to the Wasserstein metric, which is analogous to theorem 2 of Bomze (1990) and is also an approximation to answer a conjecture proposed by Oechssler and Riedel (2002).

An important issue in evolutionary games is to study the replicator dynamics as a limit of a sequence of Markov processes describing interactions among individuals in a population. These stochastic interactions describe the evolution of the species. There are many references on this issue when the strategy space is finite; for instance, to name a few, Benaim and Weibull (2003), Corradi and Sarin (2000), and Sandholm (2003, 2010). However, a more general mathematical structure is needed if the strategy set is a measurable space, which is what we propose in Section 6.

On the other hand, in the theory of evolutionary games there are several interesting dynamics, such as the imitation dynamics, the monotone-selection dynamics, the best-response dynamics, the Brown–von Neumann–Nash dynamics, and so forth (see Hofbauer and Sigmund (1998), Hofbauer and Sigmund (2003), Sandholm (2010), among others). Some of these evolutionary dynamics have been extended to games with strategies in a space of probability measures. For instance, Hofbauer et al. (2009) extend the Brown–von Neumann–Nash dynamics; Lahkar and Riedel (2015) extend the logit dynamics; and Lahkar et al. (2022) develop other related results. Moreover, Cheung (2014, 2016) proposes a general theory for pairwise comparison dynamics and for imitative dynamics. Ruijgrok and Ruijgrok (2015) extend the replicator dynamics with a mutation term. For asymmetric games, Mendoza-Palacios and Hernández-Lerma (2015) establish conditions of existence; in addition, Mendoza-Palacios and Hernández-Lerma (2015) and Narang and Shaiju (2019, 2020, 2022) define static equilibria and analyze conditions for the stability of the replicator dynamics in asymmetric games.

Among all these dynamics, we selected the replicator dynamics partly because it is the most studied for games with strategies in metric spaces, and partly because it has many interesting properties, as can be seen in Cressman (1997), Hofbauer and Weibull (1996), and many other references. In particular, with the replicator dynamics it is not difficult to construct a proof of the existence of Nash equilibria and, moreover, when the strategy set is finite, we can give a geometric characterization of the set of Nash equilibria; see Harsanyi (1973), Hofbauer and Sigmund (1998), and Ritzberger (1994).

Finally, it is noteworthy that today evolutionary games have many applications in different areas. For example, genetics and biology, Hofbauer and Sigmund (1998); modeling cancer, Gatenby and Gillies (2008), Hummert et al. (2014), Vincent and Gatenby (2005); and spread of epidemics, Bauch (2005), Yang and Yang (2015). In economics and social sciences, there are applications in different areas: in criminal behavior, Cressman et al. (1998), Quinteros and Villena (2022); corruption, Kou et al. (2021), Katsikas et al. (2016); forest management and economy of natural resources, Sethi and Somanathan (1996), Shahi and Kant (2007), Lamantia (2017); spatial economy and economic development, Fujita et al. (2001), Accinelli and Sánchez Carrera (2012), Araujo and de Souza (2010); combatting money laundering and finance, Araujo (2010), Amir et al. (2011), Amir et al. (2013); industrial organization, Bischi et al. (2015), Almudi et al. (2020c); industrial policy and innovation economics, Almudi and Fatas-Villafranca (2021), Almudi et al. (2020a), Mendoza-Palacios et al. (2022), Mendoza-Palacios and Mercado (2021), among others. We selected the examples in Section 2 because most of them are classical models in the literature of game theory and, in addition, the corresponding strategy sets are metric spaces. This allows us to relate some of our main theoretical results to interesting particular applications.

1.2 Summary

The remainder of this Element is organized as follows. Section 1.3 presents notation and technical requirements.

Section 2 introduces a normal-form game and presents important related concepts. We also show examples that will be used in the rest of this Element.

Section 3 introduces an evolutionary dynamics for asymmetric games. Section 3.1 shows a heuristic approximation to the replicator dynamics for the asymmetric case. Section 3.2 describes the asymmetric evolutionary game and the replicator dynamics. Section 3.3 establishes conditions for the existence of a solution to the system of differential equations describing the replicator dynamics, and gives some characterizations of the solution. Section 3.4 establishes a relationship between *Nash equilibria* and the replicator dynamics. Section 3.5 introduces conditions to establish the stability of the replicator equations. Section 3.6 proposes examples to illustrate our results. We conclude the section in Section 3.7 with some general comments on possible extensions.

Section 4 introduces an evolutionary dynamics for symmetric games. Section 4.1 describes the replicator dynamics and its relation to evolutionary games. Some important technical issues are also summarized. Section 4.2 establishes the relation between the replicator dynamics and a normal-form game using the concepts of Nash equilibria and *strongly uninvadable strategies*. Section 4.3 presents a brief review of stability results for the replicator dynamics. Section 4.4 establishes an important relationship between Nash equilibria and the critical points of the replicator dynamics. Section 4.5 proposes examples to illustrate our results. Finally, we conclude in Section 4.6 with some general comments on possible extensions of our results.

Section 5 proposes approximation schemes for the replicator dynamics in measure spaces, including the approximation by dynamical systems in finite-dimensional spaces (see Section 5.1). Section 5.2 presents an approximation theorem in the strong form, using the variational norm; and Section 5.3 presents an approximation theorem in the weak form, using the Kantorovich–Rubinstein norm. Section 5.4 illustrates with some examples our results. Finally, we conclude in Section 5.5 with some comments on other possible approximations.

Section 6 studies the replicator dynamics as a limit of a sequence of Markov processes. Section 6.1 presents notation and technical requirements. Section 6.2 shows a technique proposed by Kolokoltsov (2006, 2010) to approximate a sequence of pure jump models of binary interaction (in a Banach space), via a deterministic dynamical system. Section 6.3 uses techniques of Section 6.2 to establish conditions under which the replicator dynamics are the limit of a sequence of Markov processes.

Section 7 presents a summary of contributions and future perspectives. Finally, the online appendix (available at www.cambridge.org/evolutionary-games) contains facts on metrics on spaces of probability measures, and the proof of some technical results.

1.3 Technical Preliminaries

1.3.1 Spaces of Signed Measures

Consider a separable metric space A and its Borel σ-algebra $\mathcal{B}(A)$. Let $\mathbb{M}(A)$ be the Banach space of finite signed measures μ on $\mathcal{B}(A)$ endowed with the total variation norm

$$\|\mu\| := \sup_{\|f\|\leq 1} \left| \int_A f(a)\mu(da) \right| = |\mu|(A), \tag{1}$$

where $|\mu| = \mu^+ + \mu^-$ denotes the total variation of μ, and μ^+, μ^- stand for the positive and negative parts of μ, respectively. The supremum in (1) is taken over functions in the Banach space $\mathbb{B}(A)$ of real-valued bounded measurable functions on A, endowed with the supremum norm

$$\|f\| := \sup_{a\in A} |f(a)|. \tag{2}$$

Consider the subset $\mathbb{C}_B(A) \subset \mathbb{B}(A)$ of all real-valued continuous and bounded functions on A, and the dual pair $(\mathbb{C}_B(A), \mathbb{M}(A))$ given by the bilinear form $\langle \cdot, \cdot \rangle \colon \mathbb{C}_B(A) \times \mathbb{M}(A) \to \mathbb{R}$

$$\langle g, \mu \rangle := \int_A g(a)\mu(da). \tag{3}$$

We consider the *weak topology* on $\mathbb{M}(A)$ (induced by $\mathbb{C}_B(A)$), that is, the topology under which the elements of $\mathbb{C}_B(A)$, when regarded as linear functionals

$\langle g, \cdot \rangle$ on $\mathbb{M}(A)$, are continuous. In this topology a neighborhood of a point $\mu \in \mathbb{M}(A)$ is of the form

$$\mathcal{V}_\epsilon^{\mathcal{H}}(\mu) := \left\{ \nu \in \mathbb{M}(A): \; |\langle g, \nu - \mu \rangle| < \epsilon \;\; \forall g \in \mathcal{H} \right\} \tag{4}$$

for $\epsilon > 0$ and $\mathcal{H}$ a finite subset of $\mathbb{C}_B(A)$.

Definition 1 *A sequence of measures $\mu_n \in \mathbb{M}(A)$ is said to be* weakly convergent *if there exists $\mu \in \mathbb{M}(A)$ such that*

$$\lim_{n \to \infty} \int_A g(a) \mu_n(da) = \int_X g(a) \mu(da) \tag{5}$$

for all g in $\mathbb{C}_B(A)$. If $\mathbb{M}(A)$ is replaced by the space $\mathbb{P}(A)$ of probability measures on A, sometimes we say that μ_n converges in distribution to μ.

1.3.2 Metrics on $\mathbb{P}(A)$

There are many metrics that metrize the weak topology. The following metrics are particularly useful. (For details see, for instance, Shiryaev (1996), Billingsley (2013), or Villani (2008)). This subsection will be used in Section 4; the reader can skip it and come back to it later.

Let A be a separable metric space with a metric ϑ, and $\mathbb{P}(A)$ the set of probability measures on A. For any $\mu, \nu \in \mathbb{P}(A)$ we define the following metrics on $\mathbb{P}(A)$.

(i) **The Prokhorov metric** r_p, defined as

$$r_p(\mu, \nu) := \inf\{\alpha > 0: \; \mu(E) \leq \nu(E_\alpha) + \alpha \; \text{ and } \; \nu(E) \leq \mu(E_\alpha) + \alpha\}, \tag{6}$$

where, for $\alpha > 0$, $E_\alpha := \{a \in A: \vartheta(a, E) < \alpha\}$ if $E \neq \phi$. Here ϕ is the empty set, and

$$\vartheta(a, E) := \inf\{\vartheta(a, a'): \; a' \in E\}.$$

(ii) **The bounded Lipschitz metric** r_{bl}, defined as

$$r_{bl}(\mu, \nu) := \sup_{f \in \mathbb{L}_B(A)} \left\{ \int_A f(a) \mu(da) - \int_A f(a) \nu(da): \; \|f\|_{BL} \leq 1 \right\}, \tag{7}$$

where $(\mathbb{L}_B(A), \|\cdot\|_{BL})$ is the space of bounded, continuous, and real-valued functions on A that satisfy the Lipschitz condition

$$\|f\|_L := \sup \frac{|f(a) - f(b)|}{\vartheta(a, b)} < \infty, \tag{8}$$

where the supremum is over all $a \neq b$. For any $f \in \mathbb{L}_B(A)$, the norm $||f||_{BL}$ is defined as

$$||f||_{BL} := ||f|| + ||f||_L. \tag{9}$$

(iii) **The Kantorovich–Rubinstein metric** r_{kr}, defined as

$$r_{kr}(\mu, \nu) := \sup_{f \in \mathbb{L}(A)} \left\{ \int_A f(a)\mu(da) - \int_A f(a)\nu(da) \colon ||f||_L \leq 1 \right\}, \tag{10}$$

where $(\mathbb{L}(A), ||\cdot||_L)$ is the space of continuous real-valued functions on A that satisfy the Lipschitz condition (8). Let a_0 be a fixed point in A, and

$$\mathbb{M}_K(A) := \left\{ \mu \in \mathbb{M}(A) \colon \sup_{f \in \mathbb{L}(A)} \int_A |f(a)|\mu(da) < \infty \right\}.$$

Then the Kantorovich–Rubinstein metric r_{kr} can be extended as a norm on $\mathbb{M}_K(A)$ defined as

$$||\mu||_{kr} := |\mu(A)| + \sup_{f \in \mathbb{L}(A)} \left\{ \int_A f(a)\mu(da) \colon ||f||_L \leq 1, f(a_0) = 0 \right\}, \tag{11}$$

for any μ in $\mathbb{M}_K(A)$ (see Bogachev (2007), chapter 8). Note that for any $\mu, \nu \in \mathbb{P}(A)$ $r_{kr}(\mu, \nu) = ||\mu - \nu||_{kr}$, since

$$\begin{aligned}
&\sup_{f \in \mathbb{L}(A)} \left\{ \int_A f(a)\mu(da) - \int_A f(a)\nu(da) \colon ||f||_L \leq 1 \right\} \\
&= \sup_{f \in \mathbb{L}(A)} \left\{ \int_A \big(f(a) - f(a_0)\big)\mu(da) - \int_A \big(f(a) - f(a_0)\big)\nu(da) \colon ||f||_L \leq 1 \right\} \\
&= \sup_{g \in \mathbb{L}(A)} \left\{ \int_A g(a)\mu(da) - \int_A g(a)\nu(da) \colon ||g||_L \leq 1, \ g(a_0) = 0 \right\}.
\end{aligned}$$

(iv) Let us suppose that the separable metric space A is also complete (that is, a so-called Polish space), and let a_0 be a fixed point in A. For each p with $1 \leq p < \infty$, we define the space $\mathbb{P}_p(A)$ as

$$\mathbb{P}_p(A) := \left\{ \mu \in \mathbb{P}(A) \colon \int_A [\vartheta(a, a_0)]^p \mu(da) < \infty \right\}.$$

The L^p**-Wasserstein distance** r_{w_p} between μ and ν in $\mathbb{P}_p(A)$ is defined by

$$r_{w_p}(\mu, \nu) := \left[\inf_{\pi \in \Pi} \int_A \int_A [\vartheta(a, b)]^p \pi(da, db) \right]^{\frac{1}{p}}, \tag{12}$$

where Π is the set of probability measures on $A \times A$ with marginals μ and ν. In particular, when $p = 1$, we write the L^1**-Wasserstein distance** r_{w_1} as r_w and in addition we have that $r_w = r_{kr}$ on $\mathbb{P}(A)$.

Remark 2 *In the rest of this work we will denote by* r_{w^*} **any metric that metrizes the weak topology** *on* $\mathbb{P}(A)$ *(not to be confused with the notation* r_w *of the* L^1*-Wasserstein distance). Moreover, we denote by* r **any metric on** $\mathbb{P}(A)$ *that is either the total variation norm* (1) *or any distance that metrizes the weak topology. An open ball in the metric space* $(\mathbb{P}(A), r)$ *is defined in the classical form*

$$\mathcal{V}_\alpha^r(\mu) := \left\{\nu \in \mathbb{P}(A) : r(\nu, \mu) < \alpha\right\}, \tag{13}$$

where $\alpha > 0$.

Remark 3 *Let* A *be a separable metric space, and* r_{w^*} *any distance that metrizes the weak topology* τ_{w^*} *in* $\mathbb{P}(A)$*. Let* μ *be any measure in* $\mathbb{P}(A)$*, and consider the family* $\mathcal{V}^{\mathcal{H}}(\mu)$ *of neighborhoods* $\mathcal{V}_\epsilon^{\mathcal{H}}(\mu)$ *of the form* (4)*. In addition, consider the family* $\mathcal{V}^{r_{w^*}}(\mu)$ *of the open balls* $\mathcal{V}_\alpha^{r_{w^*}}(\mu)$ *of the form* (13)*. Both families* $\mathcal{V}^{\mathcal{H}}(\mu)$ *and* $\mathcal{V}^{r_{w^*}}(\mu)$ *are* neighborhood basis *for* μ *in the space* $(\mathbb{P}(A), \tau_{w^*})$*. For details see Pedersen (2012), chapters I–II.*

Moreover, a neighborhood $\mathcal{V}_\epsilon^{\mathcal{H}}(\mu)$ *for* μ *is contained in some* open ball $\mathcal{V}_\alpha^{r_{w^*}}(\mu)$ with center μ. *The inverse is also true, that is, any open ball* $\mathcal{V}_\alpha^{r_{w^*}}(\mu)$ *is contained in some neighborhood* $\mathcal{V}_\epsilon^{\mathcal{H}}(\mu)$.

1.3.3 Product Spaces

Consider two separable metric spaces X and Y with their Borel σ-algebras $\mathcal{B}(X)$ and $\mathcal{B}(Y)$. We denote by $\sigma[X \times Y]$ the σ-algebra on $X \times Y$ generated by the Cartesian product $\mathcal{B}(X) \times \mathcal{B}(Y)$. For $\mu \in \mathbb{M}(X)$ and $\nu \in \mathbb{M}(Y)$, we denote their product by $\mu \times \nu \in \mathbb{M}(X \times Y)$.

Proposition 4 *For* $\mu \in \mathbb{M}(X)$ *and* $\nu \in \mathbb{M}(Y)$*, it holds that*

$$\|\mu \times \nu\| \leq \|\mu\|\|\nu\|. \tag{14}$$

As a consequence, $\mu \times \nu$ *is in* $\mathbb{M}(X \times Y)$.

Proof See Heidergott and Leahu (2010), lemma 4.2. □

Now consider a finite family of metric spaces $\{X_i\}_{i=1}^n$ and their σ-algebras $\mathcal{B}(X_i)$, as well as the Banach spaces $(\mathbb{M}(X_i), \|\cdot\|)$ and $(\mathbb{M}_K(X_i), \|\cdot\|_{kr})$. For $i = 1, \ldots, n$, let $\mu_i \in \mathbb{M}(X_i)$. Consider the elements $\mu = (\mu_1, \mu_2, \ldots, \mu_n)$ in the product space $\mathbb{M}(X_1) \times \mathbb{M}(X_2) \times \cdots \times \mathbb{M}(X_n)$ for which

$$\|\mu\|_\infty = \|(\mu_1, \ldots, \mu_n)\|_\infty := \max_{1 \leq i \leq n} \|\mu_i\| < \infty. \tag{15}$$

These elements form a Banach space with $\|\cdot\|_\infty$ as a norm. We call it the *direct product* of the Banach spaces $\mathbb{M}(X_i)$. We can similarly define the Banach space $(\mathbb{M}_K(X_1)\times\cdots\times\mathbb{M}_K(X_n), \|\cdot\|_\infty^{kr})$, where

$$\|\mu\|_\infty^{kr} := \max_{1\le i\le n} \|\mu_i\|_{kr} < \infty. \tag{16}$$

1.3.4 Differentiability

Definition 5 *Let A be a separable metric space. We say that a mapping $\mu\colon [0,\infty)\to\mathbb{M}(A)$ is* strongly differentiable *if there exists $\mu'(t)\in\mathbb{M}(A)$ such that, for every $t>0$,*

$$\lim_{\epsilon\to 0}\left\|\frac{\mu(t+\epsilon)-\mu(t)}{\epsilon}-\mu'(t)\right\| = 0. \tag{17}$$

Note that, by (1)*, the left-hand side in* (17) *can be expressed as*

$$\lim_{\epsilon\to 0}\sup_{\|g\|\le 1}\left|\frac{1}{\epsilon}\left[\int_A g(a)\mu(t+\epsilon,da)-\int_A g(a)\mu(t,da)\right]-\int_A g(a)\mu'(t,da)\right|.$$

The signed measure μ' in (17) *is called* strong derivative.

For weak differentiability, see Remark 47.

1.4 Comments

This section presented a general introduction and summary of this Element. In addition, some technical preliminaries to be used in the following sections were presented. The only remaining information to be included is some references addressing evolutionary games in an explicit and comprehensive manner. First, we mention references for evolutionary games with *finite* strategy spaces. Webb (2007) and Weibull (1997) are two good introductory books; Hofbauer and Sigmund (1998) and Sandholm (2010) are two books that address a larger number of topics on evolutionary games; Cressman (2003) uses techniques based on subgame decompositions of *extensive form games* to analyze convergence results for evolutionary dynamics.

Regarding books dealing with evolutionary games with measurable strategy spaces we can only mention Bomze and Pötscher (1989). Nevertheless, this book was written in 1989 and so it does not address several subsequent results that have been developed in this theory. Other references on theoretical advances of this topic are mentioned in the introduction. Most of them, however, only touch theoretical aspects, and there are few bibliographies about applications; for example, oligopoly theory, Rabanal (2017), public goods models, Rabanal (2017), and preferences economic theory, Heifetz et al. (2007) and Norman (2012).

2 Normal-Form Games

This section is organized as follows. Section 2.1 presents a normal-form game and important related concepts. The following sections show examples that will be used in the rest of this Element. Most of them are classical models in the literature of game theory and, in addition, the corresponding strategy sets are metric spaces. This allows us to relate some of our main theoretical results (in evolutionary games given in the following sections) to interesting particular applications.

Section 2.2 shows a linear-quadratic model that can be applied in many situations, such as oligopoly theory, international trade models, or public good games. Section 2.3 concerns the tragedy of the commons model which is a classical game used to describe the use of natural resources. Section 2.4 presents poverty traps that describe the possible causes of economic underdevelopment of a country. Section 2.5 shows the classical Bertrand game. Sections 2.6 and 2.7 present the graduate risk model and the war attrition game, respectively. These games describe a situation where the players compete for a resource.

2.1 Normal-form games

In this section we introduce normal-form games and define the concept of Nash equilibrium as a solution of such games.

Consider a set $I := \{1,2,\ldots,n\}$ of players. For each player $i \in I$, let A_i be the set of *pure strategies*, which is a separable metric space. Let $\mathcal{B}(A_i)$ be the Borel σ-algebra of A_i, and $\mathbb{P}(A_i)$ the set of probability measures on A_i, also known as the set of *mixed strategies*. For every $i \in I$ and every vector $a := (a_1,\ldots,a_n)$ in the Cartesian product $A := A_1 \times \cdots \times A_n$, we write a as (a_i, a_{-i}) where $a_{-i} := (a_1,\ldots,a_{i-1},a_{i+1},\ldots,a_n)$ is in $A_{-i} := A_1 \times \cdots \times A_{i-1} \times A_{i+1} \times \cdots \times A_n$. Finally, for each player i we assign a payoff function $J_i\colon \mathbb{P}(A_1) \times \cdots \times \mathbb{P}(A_n) \to \mathbb{R}$ that explains the interrelation with other players, and which is defined as

$$J_i(\mu_1,\ldots,\mu_n) := \int_{A_1} \cdots \int_{A_n} U_i(a_1,\ldots,a_n)\mu_n(da_n)\ldots\mu_1(da_1), \tag{18}$$

where $U_i\colon A_1 \times \cdots \times A_n \to \mathbb{R}$ is a given measurable function. Sometimes we call U_i a utility or payoff function.

For every $i \in I$ and every vector $\mu := (\mu_1,\ldots,\mu_n)$ in $\mathbb{P}(A_1) \times \cdots \times \mathbb{P}(A_n)$, we write μ as (μ_i, μ_{-i}), where $\mu_{-i} := (\mu_1,\ldots,\mu_{i-1},\mu_{i+1},\ldots,\mu_n)$ is in

$$\mathbb{P}(A_1) \times \cdots \times \mathbb{P}(A_{i-1}) \times \mathbb{P}(A_{i+1}) \times \cdots \times \mathbb{P}(A_n).$$

If δ_{a_i} is a Dirac probability measure concentrated at $a_i \in A_i$, the vector (δ_{a_i}, μ_{-i}) is written as (a_i, μ_{-i}), and so

$$J_i(\delta_{a_i}, \mu_{-i}) = J_i(a_i, \mu_{-i}). \tag{19}$$

It is convenient to rewrite (18) as

$$\mathcal{I}_{(\mu_1,\ldots,\mu_n)} U_i := \int_{A_1} \cdots \int_{A_n} U_i(a_1, \ldots, a_n)\mu_n(da_n) \ldots \mu_1(da_1). \tag{20}$$

Hence (19) becomes

$$\begin{aligned} J_i(a_i, \mu_{-i}) &= \int_{A_{-i}} U_i(a_i, a_{-i})\mu_{-i}(da_{-i}) \\ &= \mathcal{I}_{(\mu_1,\ldots,\mu_{i-1},\mu_{i+1},\ldots,\mu_n)} U_i(a_i). \end{aligned} \tag{21}$$

In particular, (18) yields

$$J_i(\mu_i, \mu_{-i}) := \int_{A_i} J_i(a_i, \mu_{-i})\mu_i(da_i). \tag{22}$$

Finally, a *normal-form game* Γ can be described as

$$\Gamma := \left[I, \left\{ \mathbb{P}(A_i) \right\}_{i\in I}, \left\{ J_i(\cdot) \right\}_{i\in I} \right], \tag{23}$$

where

(*i*) $I = \{1, 2, \ldots n\}$ is the set of players,
(*ii*) for each player $i \in I$ we specify a set of actions (or strategies) $\mathbb{P}(A_i)$ and a payoff function $J_i \colon \mathbb{P}(A_1) \times \cdots \times \mathbb{P}(A_n) \to \mathbb{R}$.

Definition 6 *Let Γ be a normal-form game. A vector μ^* in $\mathbb{P}(A_1) \times \cdots \times \mathbb{P}(A_n)$ is called* ϵ-equilibrium *($\epsilon > 0$) if, for all $i \in I$,*

$$J_i(\mu_i^*, \mu_{-i}^*) \geq J_i(\mu_i, \mu_{-i}^*) - \epsilon \quad \forall \mu_i \in \mathbb{P}(A_i).$$

If the inequality is true when $\epsilon = 0$, then μ^* is called a Nash equilibrium.

We can obtain from (23) a *symmetric* normal-form game when $I = \{1, 2\}$, and the sets of actions and payoff functions are the same for both players, that is, $\mathbb{P}(A) = \mathbb{P}(A_1) = \mathbb{P}(A_2)$ and $J(\mu_1, \mu_2) = J_1(\mu_1, \mu_2) = J_2(\mu_2, \mu_1)$ for all $\mu_1, \mu_2 \in \mathbb{P}(A)$. Hence, we can describe a *two-player symmetric normal-form game* as

$$\Gamma_s := \left[I = \{1, 2\},\ \mathbb{P}(A),\ J(\cdot) \right]. \tag{24}$$

For symmetric normal-form games Γ_s we can express a symmetric Nash equilibrium (μ^*, μ^*) in terms of the strategy $\mu^* \in \mathbb{P}(A)$, as follows.

Definition 7 *We say that* $\mu^* \in \mathbb{P}(A)$ *is a* Nash equilibrium strategy (NES) *if the pair* (μ^*, μ^*) *is a Nash equilibrium for* Γ_s. *That is,*

$$J(\mu^*, \mu^*) \geq J(\mu, \mu^*) \quad \forall \mu \in \mathbb{P}(A). \tag{25}$$

2.2 A Linear-Quadratic Model

In this subsection we consider games in which we have two players with the following payoff functions:

$$U_1(x,y) = -a_1x^2 - b_1xy + c_1x + d_1y, \tag{26}$$

$$U_2(x,y) = -a_2y^2 - b_2yx + c_2y + d_2x, \tag{27}$$

with $a_1, a_2, b_1, b_2, c_1, c_2 > 0$ and d_1, d_2 any real numbers. Consider the strategy sets $A_1 = [0, M_1]$ and $A_2 = [0, M_2]$ for $M_1, M_2 > 0$ and large enough.

This class of games could represent a Cournot duopoly or models of international trade with linear demand and linear cost (see, for example, Varian (1992)). It can also represent some models of public good games (see Mas-Colell et al. (1995)).

If the numbers

$$(2a_2c_1 - b_1c_2),\ (2a_1c_2 - b_2c_1),\ (4a_1a_2 - b_1b_2)$$

are all positive, then we have an interior Nash equilibrium

$$(x^*, y^*) = \left(\frac{2a_2c_1 - b_1c_2}{4a_1a_2 - b_1b_2}, \frac{2a_1c_2 - b_2c_1}{4a_1a_2 - b_1b_2} \right). \tag{28}$$

2.3 The Tragedy of the Commons

The tragedy of the commons is a game where the payoff of each player depends on the use of a unique resource that must be shared. There are a variety of applications of this model, for example: (a) overfishing, the population of fish in the ocean is a shared resource; (b) the expansion of the tree population in a forest area; (c) car traffic congestion, public roads are an example of common property shared by many people; (d) use of groundwater, many cities and companies share a groundwater aquifer that is regional; (e) atmospheric pollution of a city or between cities, the atmosphere is another resource that everyone uses. In the following example the common good is a network bandwidth.

Consider a set of firms $I := \{1, 2, \ldots, n\}$ and suppose that each firm $i \in I$ wants to send and share x_i amount of data, for example audiovisual content in an internet network (as the social media firms). Assume that the network bandwidth, or the maximum capacity of the network to transmit data in a given mount of time is $\bar{x}$. Since the firm gets a payment to share its data, ideally, each of them would like to submit as much data as possible. The problem is that the quality of the network deteriorates as it is used, and if the network is overused the firms can no longer transmit data. Let $\hat{x} := x_1 + \cdots + x_n$, and assume that the value of the submitted data is given by a function $v\colon [0,\bar{x}] \to \mathbb{R}$ such that

(*i*) $v(\hat{x}) > 0$ for $0 \le \hat{x} < \bar{x}$ and $v(\hat{x}) = 0$ for $\bar{x} \le \hat{x}$;
(*ii*) $v(\cdot)$ is a concave function with the following property: $v'(\hat{x}) < 0$ and $v''(\hat{x}) < 0$ for $\hat{x} \in [0,\bar{x}]$.

Let $A_i := [0,\bar{x}]$ be the space of pure strategies of firm i. The cost of the firm i to share a unit of data is c_i, and the payoff, or benefit, of firm i is given by

$$U_i(x_i,x_{-i}) = x_i v(x_1 + \cdots + x_i + \cdots + x_n) - c_i x_i, \tag{29}$$

where $x_{-i} = (x_1,\ldots,x_{i-1},x_{i+1},\ldots,x_n)$.

Note, that $v(\cdot)$ is strictly concave (since $v'' < 0$). Then for each i in I and fixed x'_{-i}, the map $x_i \mapsto v(x'_1+\cdots+x_i+\cdots+x'_n)$ is strictly concave. Consequently, the map $x_i \mapsto U_i(x_i,x'_{-i})$ is also strictly concave. Since for each i in I, A_i is convex and compact, then there exists a unique Nash equilibrium $(x^*_1,\ldots,x^*_n)$ for the game (see Rosen (1965)).

This Nash equilibrium maximizes $U_i(\cdot,x^*_{-i})$ for each i in I and satisfies the first-order condition

$$v(x^*_1 + \cdots + x_i + \cdots + x^*_n) + x_i v'(x^*_1 + \cdots + x_i + \cdots + x^*_n) - c_i = 0. \tag{30}$$

On the other hand, the so-called social optimum, denoted by $\hat{x}^{**}$, solves

$$\max_{\hat{x}\in[0,\bar{x}]} \{\hat{x}v(\hat{x}) - \hat{x}k\},$$

where $k = \min\{c_1,\ldots,c_n\}$. Then the social optimum $\hat{x}^{**}$ satisfies the first-order condition

$$v(\hat{x}) + \hat{x}v'(\hat{x}) - k = 0. \tag{31}$$

Let $\hat{x}^* = x^*_1 + \cdots + x^*_n$. If $\hat{x}^* \le \hat{x}^{**}$ and since $v' < 0$ and $v'' < 0$, then $0 < v(\hat{x}^{**}) \le v(\hat{x}^*)$ and $v'(\hat{x}^{**}) \le v'(\hat{x}^*) < 0$. Since $x^*_i \le \hat{x}^{**}$, then the left-hand side of (30) is strictly greater than the left-hand side of (31), which is a contradiction. Therefore, comparing (30) to (31) shows that $\hat{x}^* > \hat{x}^{**}$, that is, the common resource is overutilized in the Nash equilibrium. This motivates the name tragedy of the commons.

Table 1 A poverty trap game

Worker\Firm	m	τ
s	$w_m + p - e,\ I_{s,m} - w_m - p$	$w_\tau - e,\ I_{s,\tau} - w_\tau$
a	$w_m,\ I_{a,m} - w_m$	$w_\tau,\ I_{a,\tau} - w_\tau$

2.4 A Poverty Trap Model

This section is an abbreviated version of the model proposed by Accinelli and Sánchez Carrera (2012). For related works on industrialization and poverty traps with evolutionary dynamics, see, for example, Mendoza-Palacios et al. (2022) and Mendoza-Palacios and Mercado (2021). Consider an economy with two populations, workers and firms. Each firm has two possible strategies: to be a modern firm (m) or a traditional firm (τ). A modern firm is a technological company that needs specialist workers to work in optimal conditions.

Similarly, each worker has two possible strategies: to be a specialist worker (s) or to be an artisan worker (a). A specialist worker has to spend $e > 0$ by concept of education.

The modern company pays $w_m > 0$ by finished product to any type of worker and a premium $p > e$ to specialist workers. On the other hand, a traditional firm pays $w_\tau < w_m$ by finished product. The income of each firm is determined by the workers' productivity. We will denote by $I_{f,w}$, the income of firm type $f \in \{m, \tau\}$ that employs workers type $w \in \{s, a\}$. Assume that $I_{s,m} - I_{s,\tau} > w_m + p - w_\tau$ and $w_m - w_\tau > I_{a,m} - I_{a,\tau}$.

In addition, suppose that each company uses a unique type of worker and each worker is employed in one type of firm only. The payoffs for the game are in Table 1.

Under the preceding hypotheses we have two pure Nash equilibria (s, m), (a, τ) and one Nash equilibrium in mixed strategies (μ^*, ν^*) where

$$\mu^*(s) = \frac{e}{p} \tag{32}$$

and

$$\nu^*(m) = \frac{(w_m - w_\tau) - (I_{a,\tau} - I_{a,m})}{(I_{s,m} - I_{s,\tau}) - (w_m + p - w_\tau)}. \tag{33}$$

2.5 A Sales Model as a Bertrand Game

This example is a Bertrand-duopoly model of sales (proposed by Varian (1980)), where each firm (or store) has zero marginal costs and a fixed cost

$k > 0$. We will suppose that each consumer desires to purchase, at most, one unit of the homogeneous good produced by the duopoly market and the maximum price that any consumer will pay for the good (consumer's price reservation) is $\gamma > 0$.

We suppose that there are two types of consumers: the *uninformed consumers* which choose any store randomly, and the *informed consumers* which know the whole distribution of prices, that is, they know the lowest available price. Let I be the number of informed consumers, V the number of uninformed consumers, and T the total number of consumers so $T = I + V$. We assume that the demand curve facing each firm is given by

$$q(p,z) = \begin{cases} I + \frac{V}{2} & \text{if } p < z, \\ \frac{V}{2} & \text{if } z \leq p, \end{cases} \tag{34}$$

where p is the price of the firm and z is the price of the opponent firm.

Given the demand curve (34), each firm maximizes its payoff function

$$U(p,z) = \begin{cases} p\left[I + \frac{V}{2}\right] - k & \text{if } 0 \leq p < z \leq \gamma, \\ p\frac{V}{2} - k & \text{if } 0 \leq z \leq p \leq \gamma. \end{cases} \tag{35}$$

Varian (1980, 1992) shows that this game does not have a Nash equilibrium in pure strategies, and that there exists a symmetric Nash equilibrium in mixed strategies given by the density function

$$\frac{d\mu^*(p)}{dp} = \begin{cases} \left[\frac{\gamma V}{2I}\right] p^{-2} & \text{if } \bar{p} \leq p \leq \gamma, \\ 0 & \text{otherwise}, \end{cases} \tag{36}$$

where $\bar{p} = \frac{\gamma V}{2I+V}$.

2.6 Graduated Risk Game

The graduated risk game is a symmetric game (proposed by Maynard Smith and Parker (1976)), where two players compete for a resource of value $v > 0$. Each player selects the "level of aggression" for the game. This "level of aggression" is captured by a probability distribution $x \in [0,1]$, where x is the probability that neither player is injured, and $\frac{1}{2}(1-x)$ is the probability that player one (or player two) is injured. If the player is injured, its payoff is $v - c$ (with $c > 0$), and hence the expected payoff for the player is

$$U(x,y) = \begin{cases} vy + \frac{v-c}{2}(1-y) & \text{if } y > x, \\ \frac{v-c}{2}(1-x) & \text{if } y \leq x, \end{cases} \tag{37}$$

where x and y are the "level of aggression" selected by the player and her opponent, respectively.

If $v < c$, this game has the NES (see Maynard Smith and Parker (1976), page 163) with the density function,

$$\frac{d\mu^*(x)}{dx} = \frac{\alpha - 1}{2} x^{\frac{\alpha-3}{2}}, \tag{38}$$

where $\alpha = \frac{c}{v}$. Moreover, if $c \leq v$, this game has the NES (see Maynard Smith and Parker (1976) and Bishop and Cannings (1978))

$$\mu^* = \delta_0. \tag{39}$$

2.7 War of Attrition Game

The war of attrition game was proposed by Maynard Smith (1974). In this two-player symmetric game, each player competes for a reward of value $v > 0$. Each player has a number $m > v$ of resources for the war and decides how much resources to spend to win this reward v. If a player is willing to risk more resources than the other player, then he wins the reward v and pays only the resources that the other player spends. Otherwise, the player loses the resources used during the war.

For x, y in the strategy set $A = [0, m]$ (with $v \leq m$), the payoff function is

$$U(x,y) = \begin{cases} v - y & \text{if } y < x, \\ \frac{v}{2} - y & \text{if } y = x, \\ -x & \text{if } y > x, \end{cases} \tag{40}$$

where x and y are the number of resources spent by the player and her opponent, respectively.

Using theorems 7–9 in Bishop and Cannings (1978), this game has a NES μ^* with the density function

$$\frac{d\mu^*(x)}{dx} = \begin{cases} \frac{1}{v} e^{-x/v} & \text{if } x \in \left[0, m - \frac{v}{2}\right], \\ 0, & \text{if } x \in \left(m - \frac{v}{2}, m\right), \\ \text{a weight } \delta_m \cdot e^{1/2 - m/v} & \text{at the atom } \{m\}. \end{cases} \tag{41}$$

2.8 Comments

This section introduced a normal-form game and important related concepts. It also showed examples that will be used in the rest of this work to relate our theoretical results on evolutionary games to some applications. It remains to give information about references of normal-form games.

There exist several books that introduce normal-form games, for instance, Kolokoltsov and Malafeyev (2010), Myerson (1997), Osborne and Rubinstein (1994), Gibbons (1992), and Fudenberg and Tirole (1991).

Other references on theoretical advances dealing with normal-form games with measurable strategy spaces and discontinuous payoff functions are, for instance, Glicksberg (1952), Dasgupta and Maskin (1986a), Dasgupta and Maskin (1986b), Simon (1987), and Reny (1999). Some recent references on the subject are Carmona and Podczeck (2014), Prokopovych and Yannelis (2014), Barelli and Meneghel (2013), Carbonell-Nicolau (2011), McLennan et al. (2011), and Carmona (2009).

3 Evolutionary Games: The Asymmetric Case

The theory of evolutionary dynamics in asymmetric games (or of several populations) has been developed for games where the strategy set of each player is finite, as in Balkenborg and Schlag (2007), Ritzberger and Weibull (1995), Samuelson and Zhang (1992), and Selten (1980). Nevertheless, there are well-known cases where the sets of strategies are metric spaces, such as oligopoly models and Nash bargaining games (see Cressman (2009)).

In this section we introduce an evolutionary dynamic model for asymmetric games where the strategy sets are measurable spaces (in fact, separable metric spaces). Under this hypothesis the replicator dynamics evolves in a Banach Space. We specify conditions under which the replicator dynamics have a solution. Furthermore, under suitable assumptions, a critical point of the system is stable. Some of the results of this section can be seen in Mendoza-Palacios and Hernández-Lerma (2015). Finally, some examples illustrate our results.

Section 3.1 presents a heuristic approach to the replicator dynamics in the asymmetric case. Section 3.2 describes the asymmetric evolutionary game and the replicator dynamics. Section 3.3 establishes conditions for the existence of a solution to the system of differential equations that define the replicator dynamics, and gives some characterizations of the solution (see Theorems 12 and 13, respectively). Section 3.4 establishes a relationship between the replicator dynamics and a normal-form game using the concepts of *Nash equilibrium* and *strong uninvadable profile* (see Theorems 16 and 19). Section 3.5 introduces conditions to establish the stability of the replicator dynamics (see Theorem 21). Section 3.6 proposes examples to illustrate our results. We conclude the section in Section 3.7 with some general comments on possible extensions.

3.1 A Heuristic Approach to the Replicator Dynamics

Let $I := \{1,2,\ldots,n\}$ be the set of different species (or players). Each individual of the species $i \in I$ can choose a single element a_i in a set of characteristics (strategies or actions) A_i, which is a separable metric space. For every $i \in I$ and every vector $a := (a_1, \ldots, a_n)$ in the Cartesian product $A := A_1 \times \cdots \times A_n$, we write a as (a_i, a_{-i}) where $a_{-i} := (a_1, \ldots, a_{i-1}, a_{i+1}, \ldots, a_n)$ is in

$$A_{-i} := A_1 \times \cdots \times A_{i-1} \times A_{i+1} \times \cdots \times A_n.$$

For each $i \in I$, let $\mathcal{B}(A_i)$ be the Borel σ-algebra of A_i, and $\mathbb{P}(A_i)$ the set of probability measures on A_i, also known as the set of *mixed strategies*. For each $i \in I$, let $N_i \in \mathbb{M}(A_i)$ be a positive measure such that for each E_i in $\mathcal{B}(A_i)$, $N_i(E_i)$ assigns the "number" (or mass) of individuals using pure strategies a_i in E_i. Then the total population of the species i is $N_i(A_i)$ and the proportion of individuals using strategies in E_i is

$$\mu_i(E_i) := \frac{N_i(E_i)}{N_i(A_i)}. \tag{42}$$

Indeed, when the set A_i of characteristics of the species i is not finite, it is convenient to consider the population size not as a "number of individuals" but as a measure $N_i \in \mathbb{M}(A_i)$. Then, for $i \in I$, we can introduce a probability measure $\mu_i \in \mathbb{P}(A_i)$ as in (42) that assigns a population distribution over the action set A_i.

For each species i we assign a payoff function $J_i : \mathbb{P}(A_1) \times \cdots \times \mathbb{P}(A_n) \to \mathbb{R}$ that explains the interrelation with the population of other species, and which is defined as in (18).

In the dynamic case, for each i in I, the measure-valued process N_i (and consequently μ_i) depends on a time parameter $t \geq 0$. For each i in I, let γ_i^1, γ_i^2 be the background per capita birth and death rates in the population i. We assume that in any time t, the background per capita net birth rate $\gamma_i := \gamma_i^1 - \gamma_i^2$ is modified by the payoff $J_i(a_i, \mu_{-i}(t))$ for using strategy $a_i \in A_i$ and where $\mu_{-i}(t) := (\mu_1(t), \ldots, \mu_{i-1}(t), \mu_{i+1}(t), \ldots, \mu_n(t))$ is in

$$\mathbb{P}(A_1) \times \cdots \times \mathbb{P}(A_{i-1}) \times \mathbb{P}(A_{i+1}) \times \cdots \times \mathbb{P}(A_n).$$

The dynamic of measure-valued process $N_i(t)$ is determined by the rate of change of the number of individuals of the species i for every $E_i \in \mathcal{B}(A_i)$, that is

$$N_i'(t, E_i) = \gamma_i N_i(t, E_i) + N_i(t, A_i) \int_{E_i} J_i(a_i, \mu_{-i}(t)) \mu_i(t, da_i) \tag{43}$$

with some initial positive measure $N_i(0)$ in $\mathbb{M}(A_i)$. The notation $N_i'(t, E_i)$ represents the strong derivative of $N_i(t)$ in the Banach space $\mathbb{M}(A_i)$ (see Definition 5) valued at $E_i \in \mathcal{B}(A_i)$, and μ_i is a probability measure defined as in (42).

For each t in $[0, \infty)$ and i in I, the term $\int_{E_i} J_i(a_i, \mu_{-i}(t)) \mu_i(t, da_i)$ in (43) values the efficiency of the strategies a_i in the set E_i of the species i when the other species have a distribution $\mu_{-i}(t)$. Note that if $J_i(\cdot,\cdot) \equiv 0$, the solution of (43) is $N_i(t,E_i) = N_i(0,E_i)e^{\gamma_i t}$ for all $E_i \in \mathcal{B}(A_i)$ and $t \geq 0$.

Using (42), we have that

$$N_i'(t,E_i) = N_i(t,A_i)\mu_i'(t,E_i) + N_i'(t,A_i)\mu_i(t,E_i)$$

for every $E_i \in \mathcal{B}(A_i)$ and $t \geq 0$. Then for each species i

$$\mu_i'(t,E_i) = \frac{N_i'(t,E_i)}{N_i(t,A_i)} - \frac{N_i'(t,A_i)\mu_i(t,E_i)}{N_i(t,A_i)} \tag{44}$$

for every $E_i \in \mathcal{B}(A_i)$ and $t \geq 0$. Hence, using (43) in (44), for each i in I, we obtain

$$\mu_i'(t,E_i) = \int_{E_i} \left[J_i(a_i,\mu_{-i}(t)) - J_i(\mu_i(t),\mu_{-i}(t))\right]\mu_i(t,da_i) \tag{45}$$

for each E_i in $\mathcal{B}(A_i)$ and $t \geq 0$. The system of equations (45) is known as *the replicator dynamics* for the asymmetric case.

3.2 Asymmetric Evolutionary Games

In an evolutionary game, the dynamics of the strategies is determined by the solution of a system of differential equations of the form

$$\mu_i'(t) = F_i(\mu_1(t),\ldots,\mu_n(t)) \quad \forall\ i \in I,\quad t \geq 0, \tag{46}$$

with some initial condition $\mu_i(0) = \mu_{i,0}$ for each $i \in I$. The notation $\mu_i'(t)$ represents the strong derivative of $\mu_i(t)$ in the Banach space $\mathbb{M}(A_i)$ (see Definition 5). For each $i \in I$, $F_i(\cdot)$ is a mapping

$$F_i\colon \mathbb{P}(A_1)\times\cdots\times\mathbb{P}(A_n) \to \mathbb{M}(A_i).$$

Let

$$F\colon \mathbb{P}(A_1)\times\cdots\times\mathbb{P}(A_n) \to \mathbb{M}(A_1)\times\cdots\times\mathbb{M}(A_n),$$

where $F(\mu) := (F_1(\mu),\ldots,F_n(\mu))$, and consider the vector

$$\mu'(t) := (\mu_1'(t),\ldots,\mu_n'(t)).$$

Then the system (46) can be expressed as

$$\mu'(t) = F(\mu(t)), \tag{47}$$

and we can see that the system lives in the Cartesian product of signed measures

$$\mathbb{M}(A_1)\times\cdots\times\mathbb{M}(A_n),$$

which is a Banach space with norm as in (15), that is,

$$\|\mu\|_\infty = \|(\mu_1, \ldots, \mu_n)\|_\infty := \max_{i \in I} \|\mu_i\|.$$

More explicitly, we may write (46) as

$$\mu_i'(t, E_i) = F_i(\mu(t), E_i) \quad \forall\, i \in I,\ E_i \in \mathcal{B}(A_i),\ t \geq 0, \tag{48}$$

where $\mu_i'(t, E_i)$ and $F_i(\mu(t), E_i)$ are the signed-measures $\mu_i'(t)$ and $F_i(\mu(t))$ valued at $E_i \in \mathcal{B}(A_i)$.

We shall be working with a special class of asymmetric evolutionary games, which can be described as

$$\left[I, \left\{\mathbb{P}(A_i)\right\}_{i \in I}, \left\{J_i(\cdot)\right\}_{i \in I}, \left\{\mu_i'(t) = F_i(\mu(t))\right\}_{i \in I}\right], \tag{49}$$

where

(*i*) $I = \{1, \ldots, n\}$ is the set of players;
(*ii*) for each player $i \in I$ we have a set of mixed strategies $\mathbb{P}(A_i)$ and a payoff function $J_i\colon \mathbb{P}(A_1) \times \cdots \times \mathbb{P}(A_n) \to \mathbb{R}$ (as in (18)); and
(*iii*) the replicator dynamics $F_i(\mu(t))$, where

$$F_i(\mu(t), E_i) := \int_{E_i} \left[J_i(a_i, \mu_{-i}(t)) - J_i(\mu_i(t), \mu_{-i}(t))\right] \mu_i(t, da_i). \tag{50}$$

3.2.1 The Symmetric Case

We can obtain from (49) a symmetric evolutionary game (see Section 4) when $I := \{1, 2\}$ and the sets of actions and payoff functions are the same for both players, that is, $A = A_1 = A_2$ and $U(a, b) = U_1(a, b) = U_2(b, a)$, for all $a, b \in A$. As a consequence, the sets of mixed actions and the expected payoff functions are the same for both players, that is, $\mathbb{P}(A) = \mathbb{P}(A_1) = \mathbb{P}(A_2)$ and $J(\mu, \nu) = J_1(\mu, \nu) = J_2(\nu, \mu)$, for all $\mu, \nu \in \mathbb{P}(A)$. This kind of model determines the dynamic interaction of strategies of a unique species through the replicator dynamics $\mu'(t) = F(\mu(t))$, where $F\colon \mathbb{P}(A) \to \mathbb{M}(A)$ is given by

$$F(\mu(t), E) := \int_E \left[J(a, \mu(t)) - J(\mu(t), \mu(t))\right] \mu(t, da) \quad \forall E \in \mathcal{B}(A). \tag{51}$$

Finally, as in (49), we can describe a symmetric evolutionary game as

$$[I = \{1, 2\},\ \mathbb{P}(A),\ J(\cdot),\ \mu'(t) = F(\mu(t))]. \tag{52}$$

3.2.2 Another Approach to Asymmetric Games

Bomze and Pötscher (1989) suggest an approach in which asymmetric games are reduced to symmetric ones. They construct a new strategy set $\bar{A}$ and a new payoff function J: $\bar{A} \times \bar{A} \to \mathbb{R}$. The strategy set $\bar{A}$ decomposes into mutually disjoint sets A_i, that is, $\bar{A} := \cup_{i \in I} A_i$, where A_i is the set of strategies of the species $i \in I$. Then any measurable set $E \subset \bar{A}$ may be expressed as a union of mutually disjoint sets E_i, that is, $E = \cup_{i \in I} E_i$, where $E_i = E \cap A_i$. Hence $\mu(E) = \sum_{i \in I} \mu(E_i) = \sum_{i \in I} \mu_i(E)\mu(A_i)$, where

$$\mu_i(E) := \mu(E|A_i) = \frac{\mu(E \cap A_i)}{\mu(A_i)}. \tag{53}$$

The new payoff function is given by

$$J(\mu, \nu) = \sum_{i \in I} \mu(A_i) J_i(\mu_i, \nu_{-i}),$$

where $\nu_{-i} := (\nu_1, \ldots, \nu_{i-1}, \nu_{i+1}, \ldots, \nu_n)$ with μ_i (and each ν_j in ν_{-i}) as in (53) and $J_i(\mu_i, \nu_{-i})$ as in (18).

The replicator dynamics is constructed as in the symmetric case (51), with

$$F(\mu(t), E) := \sum_{i \in I} \mu(A_i) \int_{E_i} \left[J_i(a_i, \mu_{-i}(t)) - \mu(A_i) J_i(\mu_i(t), \mu_{-i}(t)) \right] \mu_i(t, da_i).$$

3.3 Existence

In this section we introduce conditions for the existence and uniqueness of solutions to the differential system (45). For this purpose we give conditions under which the operator F in (46)–(47) is Lipschitz, when this operator is defined as in (50).

For each $i \in I$ and $t \geq 0$, let

$$\beta_i(a_i|\mu(t)) := J_i(a_i, \mu_{-i}(t)) - J_i(\mu_i(t), \mu_{-i}(t)). \tag{54}$$

Hence, by (50), $\beta_i(\cdot|\mu(t))$ is the Radon–Nikodym density of $F_i(\mu(t))$ with respect to $\mu_i(t)$, that is,

$$F_i(\mu(t), E_i) = \int_{E_i} \beta_i(a_i|\mu(t)) \mu_i(t, da_i) \quad \forall E_i \in \mathcal{B}(A_i). \tag{55}$$

Remark 8 *(i) We will use the usual notation $\mu \ll \nu$ to indicate that μ is absolutely continuous respect to ν (i.e. for every set $E \in \mathcal{B}(A)$ with $\nu(E) = 0$ we have $\mu(E) = 0$).*

(ii) Let A be a separable metric space with Borel σ-algebra $\mathcal{B}(A)$. Suppose that $\nu, \eta \in \mathbb{M}(A)$ and $c_1, c_2 \geq 0$, and let $\mu = c_1\eta + c_2\nu$. If there exists a positive

measure $\kappa \in \mathbb{M}(A)$ such that $\nu \ll \kappa$ and $\eta \ll \kappa$, then also $\mu \ll \kappa$. Moreover, the Radon–Nikodym densities

$$\varphi_{\nu\kappa} = \frac{d\nu}{d\kappa} \text{ and } \varphi_{\eta\kappa} = \frac{d\eta}{d\kappa},$$

are such that

$$\varphi_{\mu\kappa} = \frac{d\mu}{d\kappa} = c_1\varphi_{\eta\kappa} + c_2\varphi_{\nu\kappa}.$$

Lemma 9 *Let ν, η, μ, κ, and $\varphi_{\mu\kappa}$ be as in Remark 8. Then the total variation norm of μ is given by*

$$\|\mu\| = \int_A |\varphi_{\mu\kappa}(a)|\kappa(da).$$

In particular, the distance between the signed measures ν and η is given by

$$\|\nu - \eta\| = \int_A |(\varphi_{\nu\kappa} - \varphi_{\eta\kappa})(a)|\kappa(da).$$

The following proposition extends to our context some results by Bomze (1991) (lemma 1) and Oechssler and Riedel (2001) (lemma 3) in the case of symmetric evolutionary games.

Theorem 10 *Suppose that, for each $i \in I$, the function $\beta_i(\cdot|\mu)$ in (54) satisfies:*

(i) there exists $C_i \geq 0$ such that $|\beta_i(a_i|\mu)| \leq C_i$ for each $a_i \in A_i$ and $\|\mu\|_\infty \leq 2$;
(ii) there is a constant $D_i > 0$ such that

$$\sup_{a_i \in A_i} |\beta_i(a_i|\eta) - \beta_i(a_i|\nu)| \leq D_i\|\eta - \nu\|_\infty$$

for each ν, η with $\|\eta\|_\infty, \|\nu\|_\infty \leq 2$.

Then there exists a bounded Lipschitz map

$$G\colon \mathbb{M}(A_1) \times \cdots \times \mathbb{M}(A_n) \to \mathbb{M}(A_1) \times \cdots \times \mathbb{M}(A_n),$$

which coincides with F on $\mathbb{P}(A_1) \times \cdots \times \mathbb{P}(A_n)$.

Proof For each $i \in I$ and ν, η with $\|\eta\|_\infty, \|\nu\|_\infty \leq 2$, let $\mu_i = \frac{|\eta_i|+|\nu_i|}{2}$. Then $\|\mu_i\| \leq 2$, $\eta_i \ll \mu_i$ and $\nu_i \ll \mu_i$. Whence there exist the Radon–Nikodym densities $\frac{d\eta_i}{d\mu_i} = \varphi_{\eta_i\mu_i}$ and $\frac{d\nu_i}{d\mu_i} = \varphi_{\nu_i\mu_i}$. Using (55) and Lemma 9, we have that

$$\|F_i(\eta) - F_i(\nu)\|$$
$$= \int_{A_i} \left|\beta_i(a_i|\eta)\varphi_{\eta_i\mu_i}(a_i) - \beta_i(a_i|\nu)\varphi_{\nu_i\mu_i}(a_i)\right| \mu_i(da_i)$$

$$
\begin{aligned}
&\leq \int_{A_i} \Big|\beta_i(a_i|\eta) - \beta_i(a_i|\nu)\Big| \Big|\varphi_{\eta_i\mu_i}(a_i)\Big| \mu_i(da_i) \\
&\quad + \int_{A_i} \Big|\beta_i(a_i|\nu)\Big| \Big|\varphi_{\eta_i\mu_i}(a_i) - \varphi_{\nu_i\mu_i}(a_i)\Big| \mu_i(da_i) \\
&\leq \int_{A_i} \Big|\beta_i(a_i|\eta) - \beta_i(a_i|\nu)\Big| |\eta_i|(da_i) \\
&\quad + \int_{A_i} \Big|\beta_i(a_i|\nu)\Big| \Big|\varphi_{\eta_i\mu_i}(a_i) - \varphi_{\nu_i\mu_i}(a_i)\Big| \mu_i(da_i) \\
&\leq 2D_i \max_{j\in I} \|\eta_j - \nu_j\| + C_i\|\eta_i - \nu_i\| \\
&\leq K_i\|\eta - \nu\|_\infty,
\end{aligned}
$$

where $K_i := \max\{2D_i, C_i\}$. Therefore

$$
\|F(\eta) - F(\nu)\| = \max_{i\in I} \|F_i(\eta) - F_i(\nu)\| \leq K\|\eta - \nu\|_\infty,
$$

for all η, ν with $\|\eta\|_\infty, \|\nu\|_\infty \leq 2$, with $K := \max\{K_i \colon i \in I\}$. Hence, F is Lipschitz continuous on the subset of $\mathbb{M}(A_1)\times\cdots\times\mathbb{M}(A_n)$ with norm $\|\cdot\|_\infty \leq 2$.

Let us now consider the function

$$
G(\mu) := (2 - \|\mu\|_\infty)^+ F(\mu), \tag{56}
$$

with $(2 - \|\mu\|_\infty)^+ := \max\{0,\ 2 - \|\mu\|_\infty\}$. It is clear that $G(\cdot)$ is bounded and coincides with $F(\cdot)$ on $\mathbb{P}(A_1) \times \cdots \times \mathbb{P}(A_n)$. It remains to show that $G(\cdot)$ is Lipschitz.

Consider η and ν in $\mathbb{M}(A_1)\times\cdots\times\mathbb{M}(A_n)$. If $\|\eta\|_\infty, \|\nu\|_\infty \geq 2$, then (56) yields $G(\eta) = G(\nu) = 0$ and there is nothing to prove. Now, if $\|\eta\|_\infty > 2 \geq \|\nu\|_\infty$, then

$$
\|G(\eta) - G(\nu)\|_\infty = (2 - \|\nu\|_\infty)\|F(\nu)\|_\infty,
$$

and

$$
\|F(\nu)\|_\infty = \max_{j\in I} \int_{A_j} \Big|\beta_j(a_j|\nu)\Big| |\nu_j|(da_j) \leq \max_{j\in I} C_j\|\nu_j\| \leq C\|\nu\|_\infty,
$$

where $C = \max_{j\in I}\{C_j\}$. Hence

$$
\begin{aligned}
\|G(\eta) - G(\nu)\|_\infty &\leq (2 - \|\nu\|_\infty)C\|\nu\|_\infty \\
&\leq 2C(\|\eta\|_\infty - \|\nu\|_\infty) \leq 2C\|\eta - \nu\|_\infty.
\end{aligned} \tag{57}
$$

Finally, if $\|\eta\|_\infty, \|\nu\|_\infty \leq 2$, then

$$
\begin{aligned}
&\|G(\eta) - G(\nu)\|_\infty \\
&= \|(2 - \|\eta\|_\infty)F(\eta) - (2 - \|\nu\|_\infty)F(\nu)\|_\infty \\
&\leq (2 - \|\eta\|_\infty)\|F(\eta) - F(\nu)\|_\infty + \|F(\nu)\|_\infty\, \big|\|\nu\|_\infty - \|\eta\|_\infty\big| \\
&\leq 2K\|\eta - \nu\|_\infty + 2C\|\nu - \eta\|_\infty.
\end{aligned} \tag{58}
$$

Using (57) and (58) we see that, for any $\eta, \nu \in \mathbb{M}(A_1) \times \cdots \times \mathbb{M}(A_n)$, we have

$$||G(\eta) - G(\nu)||_\infty \leq 2(K + C)||\eta - \nu||_\infty. \qquad \square$$

The following proposition is an extension to our asymmetric games of lemma 4 of Oechssler and Riedel (2001) for symmetric games.

Proposition 11 *Let $i \in I$. If the payoff function $U_i(\cdot)$ is bounded, then $\beta_i(\cdot|\mu)$ satisfies the conditions (i) and (ii) of Theorem 10.*

Proof Suppose that $||\mu||_\infty \leq 2$ and let $i \in I$. Since $U_i(\cdot)$ is bounded, there exists $C'_i > 0$ such that $|U_i(a)| \leq C'_i$ for all $a \in A$. Then, by Proposition 4,

$$\begin{aligned}
|\beta_i(a_i|\mu)| &= \left| \int_{A_{-i}} U_i(a_i, a_{-i})\mu_{-i}(da_{-i}) - \int_A U_i(a)\mu(da) \right| \\
&\leq \left| \int_{A_{-i}} U_i(a_i, a_{-i})\mu_{-i}(da_{-i}) \right| + \left| \int_A U_i(a)\mu(da) \right| \\
&\leq C'_i ||\mu_1 \times \cdots \times \mu_{i-1} \times \mu_{i+1} \cdots \times \mu_n|| + C'_i ||\mu_1 \times \cdots \times \mu_n|| \\
&\leq 2^{n-1} C'_i + 2^n C'_i.
\end{aligned}$$

Letting $C_i := C'_i(2^{n-1} + 2^n)$, the condition (i) in Theorem 10 follows.

To prove the condition (ii) in Theorem 10, note that for any η and ν with $||\eta||_\infty, ||\nu||_\infty \leq 2$, using the notation in (20), and substracting and adding terms, we obtain, for every $i \in I$,

$$\begin{aligned}
&\left| \int_A U_i(a)\eta(da) - \int_A U_i(a)\nu(da) \right| \\
&\quad \leq |\mathcal{I}_{(\eta_1,\eta_2,\ldots,\eta_n)} U_i - \mathcal{I}_{(\nu_1,\eta_2,\ldots,\eta_n)} U_i| \\
&\qquad + |\mathcal{I}_{(\nu_1,\eta_2,\eta_3,\ldots,\eta_n)} U_i - \mathcal{I}_{(\nu_1,\nu_2,\eta_3,\ldots,\eta_n)} U_i| \\
&\qquad + \ldots \\
&\qquad + |\mathcal{I}_{(\nu_1,\ldots,\nu_{n-2},\eta_{n-1},\eta_n)} U_i - \mathcal{I}_{(\nu_1,\ldots,\nu_{n-2},\nu_{n-1},\eta_n)} U_i| \\
&\qquad + |\mathcal{I}_{(\nu_1,\ldots,\nu_{n-1},\eta_n)} U_i - \mathcal{I}_{(\nu_1,\ldots,\nu_{n-1},\nu_n)} U_i| \\
&\quad \leq ||U_i|| ||\eta_2 \times \cdots \times \eta_n|| ||\eta_1 - \nu_1|| \\
&\qquad + ||U_i|| ||\nu_1 \times \eta_3 \times \cdots \times \eta_n|| ||\eta_2 - \nu_2|| \\
&\qquad + \ldots \\
&\qquad + ||U_i|| ||\nu_1 \times \cdots \times \nu_{n-2} \times \eta_n|| ||\eta_{n-1} - \nu_{n-1}|| \\
&\qquad + ||U_i|| ||\nu_1 \times \cdots \times \nu_{n-1}|| ||\eta_n - \nu_n|| \\
&\quad \leq n2^{n-1} ||U_i|| \max_{j \in I} ||\eta_j - \nu_j||.
\end{aligned} \tag{59}$$

Similarly, for every $i \in I$,

$$\left| \int_{A_{-i}} U_i(a)\nu_{-i}(da_{-i}) - \int_{A_{-i}} U_i(a)\eta_{-i}(da_{-i}) \right| \leq (n-1)2^{n-2} \|U_i\| \max_{j \neq i} \|\eta_j - \nu_j\|. \tag{60}$$

Then by (59) and (60)

$$\begin{aligned} |\beta_i(a_i|\eta) - \beta_i(a_i|\nu)| &= \left| \int_{A_{-i}} U_i(a)\eta_{-i}(da_{-i}) - \int_A U_i(a)\eta(da) \right. \\ &\quad \left. - \int_{A_{-i}} U_i(a)\nu_{-i}(da_{-i}) + \int_A U_i(a)\nu(da) \right| \\ &\leq \left| \int_{A_{-i}} U_i(a)\eta_{-i}(da_{-i}) - \int_{A_{-i}} U_i(a)\nu_{-i}(da_{-i}) \right| \\ &\quad + \left| \int_A U_i(a)\nu(da) - \int_A U_i(a)\eta(da) \right| \\ &\leq n2^n \|U_i\| \max_{j \in I} \|\eta_j - \nu_j\|. \end{aligned}$$

To conclude, the latter inequality yields

$$\sup_{a_i \in A_i} |\beta_i(a_i|\eta) - \beta_i(a_i|\nu)| \leq D_i \|\eta - \nu\|_\infty,$$

with $D_i = n2^n \|U_i\|$. □

By Theorem 10, the differential equation

$$\mu'(t) = G(\mu(t)), \tag{61}$$

with G as in (56) has a unique solution in the space $\mathbb{M}(A_1) \times \cdots \times \mathbb{M}(A_n)$ (see Lang (1995), chapter IV). If $\mu(t)$ is a solution to (61) and

$$\mu(t) \in \mathbb{P}(A_1) \times \cdots \times \mathbb{P}(A_n) \quad \forall t \geq 0,$$

then $\mu(t)$ is also a solution of the differential equation (47), and it is unique since $F(\cdot)$ is Lipschitz in the open ball

$$V_2(0) = \{\mu \in \mathbb{M}(A_1) \times \cdots \times \mathbb{M}(A_n) \colon \|\mu\|_\infty < 2\}.$$

Let $\mu(\cdot)$ be a solution of (61) (or (47)). We say that a set $C \subset \mathbb{M}(A_1) \times \cdots \times \mathbb{M}(A_n)$ is an *invariant* set for (61) (or (47)), if $\mu(t)$ is in C for all $t > 0$ when $\mu(0)$ is in C.

The following proposition ensures that the set $\mathbb{P}(A_1) \times \cdots \times \mathbb{P}(A_2)$ is an invariant set for (61). Therefore the replicator dynamics has a solution.

Theorem 12 *If $\mu(t)$ is a solution to* (61)*, with initial condition $\mu(0)$ in $\mathbb{P}(A_1) \times \cdots \times \mathbb{P}(A_n)$, then $\mu(t)$ remains in $\mathbb{P}(A_1) \times \cdots \times \mathbb{P}(A_n)$ for all $t > 0$. Moreover,*

$\mu(t)$ is also the unique solution to the replicator dynamics (47) *with $F(\cdot)$ as in* (50).

Proof First, note that

$$\frac{d\mu_i(t,E_i)}{dt} = \mu'(t,E_i) \quad \forall i \in I,\ E_i \in \mathbb{B}(A_i),\ t \geq 0. \tag{62}$$

Indeed,

$$\begin{aligned}
&\left|\frac{d\mu_i(t,E_i)}{dt} - \mu_i'(t,E_i)\right| \\
&= \lim_{\epsilon\to 0}\left|\frac{\mu_i(t+\epsilon,E_i) - \mu_i(t,E_i)}{\epsilon} - \mu_i'(t,E_i)\right| \\
&= \lim_{\epsilon\to 0}\left|\frac{1}{\epsilon}\left[\int_{A_i} 1_{E_i}(a_i)\mu_i(t+\epsilon,da_i) - \int_{A_i} 1_{E_i}(a_i)\mu_i(t,da_i)\right]\right. \\
&\quad \left. - \int_{A_i} 1_{E_i}(a_i)\mu_i'(t,da_i)\right| \\
&\leq \lim_{\epsilon\to 0}\left\|\frac{\mu_i(t+\epsilon) - \mu_i(t)}{\epsilon} - \mu_i'(t)\right\| = 0.
\end{aligned}$$

Now, if $\mu(t)$ is a solution to (61), then by (62) and (56), for each $i \in I$, $E_i \in \mathbb{B}(A_i)$, and $t \geq 0$, we have

$$\frac{d\mu_i(t,E_i)}{dt} = (2-\|\mu(t)\|_\infty)^+\left[\int_{E_i} J_i(a_i,\mu_{-i}(t))\mu_i(t,da_i) - J_i(\mu_i(t),\mu_{-i}(t))\mu_i(t,E_i)\right].$$

In particular, for every $i \in I$,

$$\frac{d\mu_i(t,A_i)}{dt} = (2-\|\mu(t)\|_\infty)^+[1-\mu_i(t,A_i)]J_i(\mu_i(t),\mu_{-i}(t)). \tag{63}$$

We can express (63) as a system of differential equations in $\mathbb{R}^n$, say

$$\frac{d\mu_i(t,A_i)}{dt} = f_i(t,\mu_i(t,A_i)) \quad \text{for } i = 1,\ldots,n,$$

where we can see the vector $[f_i(t,\mu_i(t,A_i))]_{i\in I}$ as a function $f\colon [0,\infty)\times\mathbb{R}^n \to \mathbb{R}^n$ with

$$f(t,\mu_1(t,A_1),\ldots,\mu_n(t,A_n)) = [f_i(t,\mu_i(t,A_i))]_{i\in I}.$$

The system (63) has a critical point if $\mu_i(t,A_i) = 1$ for $i = 1,\ldots,n$ (i.e., $f(t,\mu_1(t,A_1),\ldots,\mu_n(t,A_n)) = 0$). Then, if $\mu_i(0,A_i) = 1$, we have that $\mu_i(t,A_i) = 1$ for all $t \geq 0$ and $i \in I$. Hence the set

$$B := \{\mu \in \mathbb{M}_1 \times \cdots \times \mathbb{M}_n : \ \mu_i(A_i) = 1 \ \forall i \in I\}$$

is an invariant set for (61). Moreover, if $E_i \in \mathbb{B}(A_i)$, $t' \geq 0$, and $\mu_i(t', E_i) = 0$, then by (64), $\mu_i(t, E_i) = 0$ for all $t \geq t'$. In particular for each $E_i \in \mathbb{B}(A_i)$ and $i \in I$,

$$|\mu_i(t, E_i) - \mu_i(s, E_i)| \leq \|\mu_i(t) - \mu_i(s)\| \quad \forall t, s \geq 0. \tag{64}$$

Since for each i in I the map $t \mapsto \mu_i(t)$ is continuous, then by (64) so is the map $t \mapsto \mu_i(t, E_i)$ for each $E_i \in \mathbb{B}(A_i)$. Therefore, if $\mu_i(0, E_i) \geq 0$, then we have $\mu_i(t, E_i) \geq 0$ for all $t > 0$ and $E_i \in \mathbb{B}(A_i)$. It follows that

$$\mathbb{P}(A_1) \times \cdots \times \mathbb{P}(A_n) \subset B$$

is an invariant set for the system of differential equations (61).

Finally, if $\mu(t)$ is a solution to (61) and $\mu(0)$ is in $\mathbb{P}(A_1) \times \cdots \times \mathbb{P}(A_n)$, then $\mu(t)$ is a solution to (47) and, since F is Lipschitz for all μ with $\|\mu\|_\infty \leq 2$, this solution is unique. □

Theorem 13 *Suppose that the conditions* (*i*) *and* (*ii*) *of Theorem 10 are satisfied. If* $\mu(t)$ *is a solution to* (47) *with the initial condition* $\mu(0)$ *in* $\mathbb{P}(A_1) \times \cdots \times \mathbb{P}(A_1)$, *then:*

(*i*) *for every* $i \in I$ *and* $t > 0$, *if* μ_i *is in* $\mathbb{P}(A_i)$, *then* $\mu_i(0) \ll \mu_i(t)$ *and* $\mu_i(t) \ll \mu_i(0)$, *with Radon–Nikodym density*

$$\frac{d\mu_i(t)}{d\mu_i(0)}(a_i) = e^{\int_0^t \beta_i(a_i|\mu(s))ds}. \tag{65}$$

(*ii*) *In particular, for every* $i \in I$ *and* $t > 0$, *if* ν_i *is a probability measure satisfying that* $\nu_i \ll \mu_i(t)$ *whenever* $\nu_i \ll \mu_i(0)$, *then*

$$\log \frac{d\nu_i}{d\mu_i(t)}(a_i) = \log \frac{d\nu_i}{d\mu_i(0)}(a_i) - \int_0^t \beta_i(a_i|\mu(s))ds. \tag{66}$$

Proof The following proof is an adaptation of Ritzberger (1994) (lemma 2) and Bomze (1991) (lemma 2). Let $\mu(t)$ be the solution to (47), with $\mu(0) \in \mathbb{P}(A_i)$ and

$$\varphi_i(t, a_i) := e^{\int_0^t \beta_i(a_i|\mu(s))ds} \geq 0 \qquad \forall i \in I. \tag{67}$$

In addition, let

$$\tilde{\mu}_i(t, E_i) := \int_{E_i} \varphi_i(t, a_i)\mu_i(0, da_i) \quad \forall E_i \in \mathcal{B}(A_i),$$

and, by (55),

$$F_i(\tilde{\mu}_i(t), E_i) = \int_{E_i} \beta_i(a_i|\mu(t))\tilde{\mu}_i(t, da_i).$$

We will prove that

$$\|\tilde{\mu}'(t) - F(\tilde{\mu}(t))\|_\infty = 0,$$

where $\tilde{\mu}'(t) = (\tilde{\mu}_1'(t), \ldots, \tilde{\mu}_n'(t))$ and $F(\tilde{\mu}(t)) = (F_1(\tilde{\mu}(t)), \ldots, F_n(\tilde{\mu}(t)))$.

Let $i \in I$ and fix $t > 0$. Then

$$\begin{aligned}
&\|\tilde{\mu}_i'(t) - F_i(\tilde{\mu}(t))\| \\
&\quad = \lim_{h\to 0} \sup_{\|g\|\leq 1} \left| \frac{1}{h} \int_{A_i} g(a_i)[\varphi_i(t+h, a_i) - \varphi_i(t, a_i)]\mu(0, da_i) \right. \\
&\qquad \left. - \int_{A_i} g(a_i)\beta_i(a_i|\mu(t))\varphi(t, a_i)\mu_i(0, da_i) \right| \\
&\quad \leq \lim_{h\to 0} \int_{A_i} \left| \frac{1}{h}[\varphi_i(t+h, a_i) - \varphi_i(t, a_i)] - \beta_i(a_i|\mu(t))\varphi_i(t, a_i) \right| \mu_i(0, da_i)
\end{aligned}$$

which, by (67),

$$\begin{aligned}
&\leq \sup_{a_i \in A_i} \left| e^{\int_0^t \beta_i(a_i|\mu(s))ds} \right| \lim_{h\to 0} \int_{A_i} \left| \frac{e^{\int_t^{t+h} \beta_i(a_i|\mu(s))ds} - 1}{h} - \beta_i(a_i|\mu(t)) \right| \mu_i(0, da_i) \\
&\leq \sup_{a_i \in A_i} \left| e^{tC_i} \right| \int_{A_i} \left| \lim_{h\to 0} \frac{e^{\int_t^{t+h} \beta_i(a_i|\mu(s))ds} - 1}{h} - \beta_i(a_i|\mu(t)) \right| \mu_i(0, da_i) = 0,
\end{aligned}$$

where the latter equality follows from the conditions (*i*) and (*ii*) of Theorem 10 together with the dominated convergence theorem. To conclude:

$$\|\tilde{\mu}'(t) - F(\tilde{\mu}(t))\|_\infty = 0 \quad \forall t > 0.$$

By the uniqueness in corollary 1.7, page 72 of Lang (1995) we thus get (65), and therefore

$$\mu_i(t) \ll \mu_i(0) \quad \forall i \in I.$$

By the condition (*ii*) of Theorem 10, for each $i \in I$ and $t > 0$, there exists $C_i \geq 0$ such that $-tC_i \leq \int_0^t \beta_i(a_i|\mu(s)) \leq tC_i$. Consequently,

$$0 < e^{-tC_i} \leq e^{\int_0^t \beta_i(a_i|\mu(s))} \leq e^{tC_i}.$$

Hence, by (65),

$$\int_{E_i} e^{-tC_i}\mu_i(0, da_i) \leq \int_{E_i} \left[e^{\int_0^t \beta_i(a_i|\mu(s))} \right] \mu_i(0, da_i) = \mu_i(t, E_i);$$

thus $\mu_i(0) \ll \mu_i(t)$.

The assertion (*ii*) follows from (*i*) and an application of the chain rule for Radon–Nikodym densities (see Bartle (1995), chapter 8). □

3.4 Nash Equilibria and the Replicator Equation

In this section we consider a normal-form game Γ as in (23), and an asymmetric evolutionary game as in (49). We wish to study the relation between a Nash equilibrium of the normal-form game Γ and the replicator equation (see Theorem 16). We also introduce the concept of *strong uninvadable profile* (Definition 17), and its relation with *ϵ-equilibrium* (Definition 6).

The following proposition states an important fact about probability measures on separable metric spaces.

Proposition 14 *Let A be a separable metric space and μ in $\mathbb{P}(A)$. Then there is a unique closed set $S \subset A$ (called* the support of μ, *in symbols S=Supp(μ)) such that $\mu(A - S) = 0$ and $\mu(O \cap S) > 0$ for every open set O for which $O \cap S \neq \emptyset$.*

Proof See Royden (1988), page 408. □

Lemma 15 *Suppose that $\mu^* = (\mu_1^*, \ldots, \mu_n^*)$ is a Nash equilibrium of Γ, and let S_i be the support of μ_i^* for some $i \in I$. Then $J_i(a_i, \mu_{-i}^*) = J_i(\mu^*, \mu_{-i}^*)$ for all $a_i \in S_i$.*

Proof Using Proposition 14, the proof is similar to the case when the strategy sets are finite (see, e.g., Webb (2007)). □

The following theorem gives an important property, namely the relation between a Nash equilibrium of a normal-form game and the replicator equation.

Theorem 16 *Suppose that $\mu^* = (\mu_1^*, \ldots, \mu_n^*)$ is a Nash equilibrium of Γ. Then μ^* is a critical point of* (47), *that is, $F(\mu^*) = 0$, when $F(\cdot)$ is described by the replicator dynamics* (50).

Proof First note that any vector of Dirac measures $\delta_{a'} = (\delta_{a'_1}, \ldots, \delta_{a'_n})$ (sometimes called a profile of pure strategies) is a critical point of (47), since for every $E_i \in \mathcal{B}(A_i)$ and $i \in I$:

$$F_i(\delta_{a'}, E_i) = \int_{E_i} \left[J_i(a_i, \delta_{a'_{-i}}) - J_i(\delta_{a'_i}, \delta_{a'_{-i}}) \right] \delta_{a'_i}(da_i) = 0.$$

Then, if μ^* is a pure Nash equilibrium, that is, $\mu^* = \delta_{a^*}$, the theorem holds.

Suppose now that the Nash equilibrium μ^* is not pure, and let S_i^* be the support of μ_i^* for $i \in I$. By Lemma 15

$$J_i(a_i, \mu_{-i}^*) = J_i(\mu_i^*, \mu_{-i}^*) \quad \forall\, a_i \in S_i^*.$$

Therefore, for any $E_i \in \mathcal{B}(A_i)$,

$$F_i(\mu^*, E_i) = \int_{E_i} \left[J_i(a_i, \mu^*_{-i}) - J(\mu^*_i, \mu^*_{-i}) \right] \mu^*_i(da_i)$$
$$= \int_{E_i \cap S^*_i} \left[J_i(a_i, \mu^*_{-i}) - J(\mu^*_i, \mu^*_{-i}) \right] \mu^*_i(da_i) = 0.$$

□

The following definition is an extended version of strongly uninvadable strategies of symmetric games (for details see Bomze (1991)).

Definition 17 *A vector $\mu^* \in \mathbb{P}(A_1) \times \mathbb{P}(A_2) \times \cdots \times \mathbb{P}(A_n)$ is called a* strong uninvadable profile (SUP) in a set C *if μ^* is in C and the following holds. There exists $\epsilon > 0$ such that for any $\mu \in C$ with $\|\mu - \mu^*\|_\infty < \epsilon$, and every $i \in I$, $J_i(\mu^*_i, \mu_{-i}) > J_i(\mu_i, \mu_{-i})$ if $\mu_i \neq \mu^*_i$. In particular if*

$$C = \mathbb{P}(A_1) \times \mathbb{P}(A_2) \times \cdots \times \mathbb{P}(A_n),$$

then μ^* is simply called a strong uninvadable profile (SUP)*. In either case, we call ϵ the global invasion barrier.*

Lemma 18 *Let $\mu, \nu \in \mathbb{P}_1(A) \times \cdots \times \mathbb{P}(A_n)$ and $\delta > 0$. Then there exists α in $(0, 1)$ such that $\|\gamma - \mu\|_\infty \leq \delta$ if $\gamma = \alpha\nu + (1 - \alpha)\mu$.*

Proof Let $0 < \alpha < \frac{\delta}{\|\nu - \mu\|_\infty}$. Then $\|\gamma - \mu\|_\infty = \|\alpha\nu + (1 - \alpha)\mu - \mu\|_\infty = \alpha\|\nu - \mu\|_\infty < \delta$. □

As usual, the open neighborhood with center μ^* and radius $\varepsilon > 0$ is defined as

$$V_\varepsilon(\mu^*) := \{\mu \in \mathbb{P}(A_1) \times \cdots \times \mathbb{P}(A_n) \colon \|\mu - \mu^*\|_\infty < \varepsilon\}. \tag{68}$$

The following theorem gives the relation between an ϵ-equilibrium (or Nash equilibrium) and strong uninvadable profiles.

Theorem 19 *Suppose that the payoff function $U_i(\cdot)$ in* (18) *is bounded for all $i \in I$. Let μ^* be a* SUP in a set C *with global invasion barrier $\epsilon_1 > 0$. If the set $C \cap V_{\epsilon_1}(\mu^*)$ has a convex and nonempty interior, then μ^* is an ϵ_2-equilibrium of Γ, where $\epsilon_2(\cdot) > 0$ is a function of ϵ_1. Moreover, if μ^* is a* SUP*, then μ^* is a Nash equilibrium and the boundedness hypothesis on U_i is not required.*

Proof Suppose that μ^* is not an ϵ_2-equilibrium of Γ for any $\epsilon_2 > 0$. Then for $\epsilon_2 > 0$, there exists $i \in I$ and $\nu \in \mathbb{P}(A_1) \times \cdots \times \mathbb{P}(A_n)$ such that

$$J_i(\nu_i, \mu^*_{-i}) - \epsilon_2 > J(\mu^*_i, \mu^*_{-i}). \tag{69}$$

By hypothesis, $\mathcal{C} \cap V_{\epsilon_1}(\mu^*)$ has a convex and nonempty interior. Hence, by Lemma 18, there exist $\alpha_1, \alpha_2 \in [0,1]$ such that $\|\eta - \mu^*\| < \epsilon_1$, where $\eta \in \mathcal{C}$ and $\eta := (1-\alpha_1)\mu^* + \alpha_1[(1-\alpha_2)\nu + \alpha_2\kappa]$ for some κ in the interior of $\mathcal{C} \cap V_{\epsilon_1}(\mu^*)$. Since μ^* is a SUP in the set $\mathcal{C}$, $J_i(\mu_i^*, \eta_{-i}) > J_i(\eta_i, \eta_{-i})$, which implies (see Section 1 of the online appendix).

$$\begin{aligned}
&(1-\alpha_2)(1-\alpha_1)^{n-1}J_i(\mu_i^*, \mu_{-i}^*) + [(1-\alpha_2)\alpha_1]^{n-1}J_i(\mu_i^*, \nu_{-i}) \\
&\quad + [\alpha_2\alpha_1]^{n-1}J_i(\mu_i^*, \kappa_{-i})] \\
&\quad > (1-\alpha_2)(1-\alpha_1)^{n-1}J_i(\nu_i, \mu_{-i}^*) \\
&\quad - \alpha_2(1-\alpha_1)^{n-1}\left[J_i(\mu_i^*, \mu_{-i}^*) - J_i(\kappa_i, \mu_{-i}^*)\right] + O(\alpha_1).
\end{aligned} \tag{70}$$

Let $\epsilon_2^* = \left(\frac{\alpha_2}{1-\alpha_2}\right) L\epsilon_1$, where $L = 2^{n-1} \max_{i \in I} \|U_i\|$. By (59)

$$|J_i(\mu_i^*, \mu_{-i}^*) - J_i(\kappa_i, \mu_{-i}^*)| < L\epsilon_1 \leq \epsilon_2 \left(\frac{1-\alpha_2}{\alpha_2}\right) \quad \forall\, \epsilon_2 \geq \epsilon_2^*.$$

Then

$$\begin{aligned}
&(1-\alpha_2)(1-\alpha_1)^{n-1}J_i(\mu_i^*, \mu_{-i}^*) \\
&\quad + [(1-\alpha_2)\alpha_1]^{n-1}J_i(\mu_i^*, \nu_{-i}) + [\alpha_2\alpha_1]^{n-1}J_i(\mu_i^*, \kappa_{-i})] \\
&\quad > (1-\alpha_2)(1-\alpha_1)^{n-1}[J_i(\nu_i, \mu_{-i}^*) - \epsilon_2] + O(\alpha_1).
\end{aligned} \tag{71}$$

If (69) is true, there exists α_1 in $(0,1)$ sufficiently close to 0, such that equation (71) is violated. So we have that μ^* is an ϵ_2-equilibrium (for $\epsilon_2 \geq \epsilon_2^*$).

Now, suppose that μ^* is a SUP and not a Nash equilibrium of Γ. Then there exists $i \in I$ and $\nu \in \mathbb{P}(A_1) \times \cdots \times \mathbb{P}(A_n)$ such that (69) is true with $\epsilon_2 = 0$. By Lemma 18 there exist $\alpha \in [0,1]$ such that $\|\eta - \mu^*\| < \epsilon_1$ where $\eta = (1-\alpha)\mu^* + \alpha\nu$. Since μ^* is a SUP, $J_i(\mu_i^*, \eta_{-i}) > J_i(\eta_i, \eta_{-i})$. Then (see Section 1 of the online appendix)

$$\begin{aligned}
&(1-\alpha)^{n-1}J_i(\mu_i^*, \mu_{-i}^*) + (\alpha)^{n-1}\left[J_i(\mu_i^*, \nu_{-i})\right] \\
&\quad > (1-\alpha)^{n-1}\left[J_i(\nu_i, \mu_{-i}^*)\right]\Big] + O(\alpha).
\end{aligned} \tag{72}$$

If μ^* is not a Nash equilibrium, then for α in $(0,1)$ sufficiently small (72) is violated. So we have that μ^* is a Nash equilibrium. □

3.5 Stability

In this section we are interested in the stability (in the sense of Definition 20) of the differential system (47). To this end, we establish that strong uninvadable profiles (Definition 17) have some type of stability.

Definition 20 *Let μ^* be a critical point of* (13), *that is,* $F(\mu^*) = 0$.

(*i*) μ^* *is called* Lyapunov stable *if, for every* $\epsilon > 0$*, there exists* $\delta > 0$ *such that if* $\|\mu(0) - \mu^*\|_\infty < \delta$*, then* $\|\mu(t) - \mu^*\|_\infty < \epsilon$ *for all* $t > 0$.

(*ii*) μ^* *is called* weakly attracting *if it is Lyapunov stable and, in addition, there exists* $\delta > 0$ *such that if* $\|\mu(0) - \mu^*\|_\infty < \delta$*, then as* $t \to \infty$*,* $\mu_i(t) \to \mu_i^*$ *weakly for all* $i \in I$.

The following proposition is an extension to asymmetric evolutionary games of theorem 3 in Oechssler and Riedel (2001).

Theorem 21 *Suppose that the conditions* (*i*) *and* (*ii*) *of Theorem 10 hold. Let* $\delta_{a^*} = (\delta_{a_1^*}, \ldots, \delta_{a_n^*})$ *be a vector of Dirac measures, and* C *an invariant set for the differential equation* (47). *If* δ_{a^*} *is a* SUP in the set C, *then there exists* $\epsilon > 0$ *such that the set*

$$C \cap V_\epsilon(\delta_{a^*})$$

is invariant for (47). *Moreover, suppose that for all i in I, the map* $\mu \mapsto \beta_i(a_i^* | \mu)$ *is weakly continuous and the set of strategies* A_i *is a compact set. If* C *is a closed set and* $\mu(0)$ *is in* $C \cap V_\epsilon(\delta_{a^*})$*, then as* $t \to \infty$*,* $\mu(t) \to \delta_{a^*}$ *in distribution (Definition 1).*

Proof First note that the vector of Dirac measures $\delta_{a^*} = (\delta_{a_1^*}, \ldots, \delta_{a_n^*})$ is a critical point of (47) (see the proof of Theorem 16). Then, if $\mu(0) = \delta_{a^*}$, we have that $\mu(t) = \delta_{a^*}$ for all $t > 0$ and the theorem holds.

Since δ_{a^*} is a SUP in the set C, there exists $\epsilon > 0$ such that for every $\mu \in C$ with $\|\mu - \delta_{a^*}\|_\infty < \epsilon$ and every $i \in I$, $J_i(\delta_{a_i^*}, \mu_{-i}) > J_i(\mu_i, \mu_{-i})$ *if* $\mu_i \neq \delta_{a_i^*}$.

Suppose that $\mu(0) \neq \delta_{a^*}$ and that $\mu(0)$ is in $C \cap V_\epsilon(\delta_{a^*})$. By (55), for each $i \in I$ and $t \geq 0$,

$$\mu_i'(t, \{a_i^*\}) = \int_{A_i} 1_{\{a^*\}}(a_i)\beta(a_i|\mu(t))\mu_i(t, da_i) = \beta(a_i^*|\mu(t))\mu_i(t, \{a_i^*\}). \tag{73}$$

Assume that, for each i in I,

$$\mu_i'(0, \{a_i^*\}) = \beta(a_i^*|\mu(0))\mu_i(0, \{a_i^*\}) > 0,$$

and define

$$t_{i,0} := \inf\{t \geq 0 : \mu_i'(t, \{a_i^*\}) = 0\}. \tag{74}$$

For each i in I, the function $\beta_i(a_i^*|\mu(t))$ is Lipschitz in $\mu(t)$, and $\mu(t)$ is continuous in t; hence the map $t \to \beta_i(a_i^*|\mu(t))$ is continuous. Also $\mu_i(t, \{a_i^*\})$ is continuous in t. Then by (73) the map $t \mapsto \mu_i'(t, \{a_i^*\})$ is continuous. So for each $i \in I$

the set $\{t \geq 0 : \mu_i'(t, \{a_i^*\}) = 0\}$ is closed and $\mu_i'(t_{i,0}, \{a_i^*\}) = 0$. By (74), for any i in I

$$\mu_i'(s, \{a_i^*\}) = \beta_i(a_i^* | \mu(s))\mu_i(s, \{a_i^*\}) > 0 \quad \forall\ 0 \leq s < t_0, \tag{75}$$

where $t_0 := \min\{t_{1,0}, \ldots, t_{n,0}\}$. As a consequence of (75) we obtain

$$\mu_i(s, \{a_i^*\}) > \mu_i(0, \{a_i^*\}) > 0 \quad \forall 0 \leq s < t_0,\ i \in I. \tag{76}$$

Note that for any $\mu_i \in \mathbb{P}(A_i)$

$$\|\mu_i - \delta_{a_i^*}\| = 2(1 - \mu_i(\{a_i^*\})) \quad \forall\, i \in I. \tag{77}$$

If $\|\mu(0) - \delta_{a^*}\|_\infty < \epsilon$, then by (76) and (77) we have

$$\|\mu(s) - \delta_{a^*}\|_\infty < \epsilon \quad \forall\ 0 \leq s < t_0.$$

By continuity of $\mu(t)$ and (76) we obtain

$$\mu_i(t_0, \{a_i^*\}) \geq \mu_i(0, \{a_i^*\}) > 0 \quad \forall\ 0 \leq s < t_0,\ \ i \in I, \tag{78}$$

and by (77) and (78)

$$\|\mu_i(t_0) - \delta_{a_i^*}\|_\infty \leq \|\mu(0) - \delta_{a^*}\|_\infty < \epsilon \quad \forall\ i \in I. \tag{79}$$

Since $\mathcal{C}$ is an invariant set, by (79) we see that $\mu(t_0) \in \mathcal{C} \cap V_\epsilon(\delta_{a^*})$ and so $\beta_i(a_i^* | \mu(t_0)) > 0$ because δ_{a^*} is a SUP in the set $\mathcal{C}$. Then by (78)

$$\mu_i'(t_0, \{a_i^*\}) = \beta_i(a_i^* | \mu(t_0))\mu_i(t_0, \{a_i^*\}) > 0 \quad \forall i \in I,$$

so $t \mapsto \mu_i(t, \{a_i^*\})$ is increasing for each i in I and, moreover,

$$\mu(t) \in \mathcal{C} \cap V_\epsilon(\delta_{a^*}) \quad \forall\ t \geq 0. \tag{80}$$

By hypothesis, A_i is compact for each $i \in I$, so $\mathbb{P}(A_i)$ is compact in the weak topology (see page 186, corollary 5.7.6 in Bobrowski (2005)) for all $i \in I$. Then $\mathcal{C} \cap \mathbb{P}(A_1) \times \cdots \times \mathbb{P}(A_n)$ is compact in the product topology.

On the other hand, δ_{a^*} is a SUP in the set $\mathcal{C}$ and, by (80), $\beta_i(a_i^* | \mu(t)) > 0$ for all $t > 0$ and i in I. Moreover, by Theorem 13,

$$\mu_i(t, \{a_i^*\}) = \mu_i(0, \{a_i^*\}) e^{\int_0^t \beta_i(a_i^* | \mu(s))ds} \leq 1 \quad \forall\, i \in I,\ \ t \geq 0;$$

hence

$$\lim_{t \to \infty} \beta_i(a_i^* | \mu(t)) = 0 \quad \forall\, i \in I.$$

Finally, let $v = (v_1, \ldots, v_n) \in \mathcal{C} \cap \mathbb{P}(A_1) \times \cdots \times \mathbb{P}(A_n)$ be an accumulation point of the trajectory $\mu(t) = (\mu_1(t), \ldots, \mu_n(t))$. By (80) the distance from v to

δ_{a^*} is at most ϵ. Since δ_{a^*} is a SUP in C and the map $\mu \mapsto \beta_i(a_i^*|\mu)$ is weakly continuous, if v is such that

$$\beta_i(a_i^*|v) = J_i(a_i^*, v_{-i}) - J_i(v_i, v_{-i}) = 0 \quad \forall\, i \in I$$

yields that $\delta_{a^*} = v$, which proves that $\mu_i(t) \rightarrow \delta_{a_i^*}$ in distribution for all i in I. □

If the vector δ_{a^*} in Theorem 21 is a SUP, then we obtain the following corollary, taking $C = \mathbb{P}(A_1) \times \cdots \times \mathbb{P}(A_n)$.

Corollary 22 *Suppose that the conditions* (*i*) *and* (*ii*) *of Theorem 10 hold. Let* $\delta_{a^*} = (\delta_{a_1^*}, \ldots, \delta_{a_n^*})$ *be a vector of Dirac measures, and suppose that it is a SUP. Then* δ_{a^*} *is Lyapunov stable for the replicator dynamics. Moreover, if the map* $\mu \mapsto \beta_i(a_i^*|\mu)$ *is weakly continuous and the set of strategies* A_i *is compact for all* $i \in I$, *then* δ_{a^*} *is weakly attracting.*

Remark 23 *Note that if, for each i in I, the payoff function* $U_i(\cdot)$ *in* (18) *is continuous, then the map* $\mu \mapsto \beta_i(a_i^*|\mu)$ *is weakly continuous. This fact is of relevance because many games satisfy that* $U_i(\cdot)$ *in* (18) *is continuous.*

3.6 Examples

In evolutionary games (49) we assume that the players choose their strategies through an evolutionary dynamics (46)–(47) which explains the interaction among them. Therefore, the solution of the game is given by a trajectory $\mu(t)$ (solution of (46)–(47)) which depends on an initial profile μ_0. Under some conditions (see Theorem 21), the trajectory $\mu(t)$ is very close to a "special" NE (solution of the normal-form game Γ in (23)). In this "special" NE the strategy of each player satisfies certain conditions of dominance, and this NE is called a SUP (see Definition 17 and Theorem 19). Therefore, for each player, the replicator dynamics is searching and selecting strategies with certain dominance.

In this section we consider the examples in Sections 2.2, 2.3, and 2.4. In each case we prove that the NE of the game is also a SUP. Thus, under the replicator dynamics if the initial profile μ_0 is close to the NE (which is a SUP), then the players select a profile $\mu(t)$ very close to the NE for every $t > 0$.

3.6.1 A Linear-Quadratic Model

Consider the game in Section 2.2. We will prove that the Nash equilibrium (28) is a SUP for the game. Let $U_1(x,y)$ and $U_2(x,y)$ be as in (26) and (27), respectively.Let

$$C_1 := \{(\mu,\nu) \in \mathbb{P}(A_1)\times\mathbb{P}(A_2) \colon \mu(x^*,M_1] = \nu(y^*,M_2] = 0\},$$
$$C_2 := \{(\mu,\nu) \in \mathbb{P}(A_1)\times\mathbb{P}(A_2) \colon \mu[0,x^*) = \nu[0,y^*) = 0\},$$

and $C = C_1 \cup C_2$. The set C is invariant for the replicator dynamics (47) and $(\delta_{x^*},\delta_{y^*})$ is in C. On the other hand, let

$$\bar{x}^\mu := \int_{A_1} x\mu(dx), \qquad \bar{y}^\nu := \int_{A_2} y\nu(dy).$$

If (μ,ν) is in C_1, then by Jensen's inequality

$$J_1(\delta_{x^*},\nu) = \int_{A_2} U_1(x^*,y)\nu(dy) = U_1(x^*,\bar{y}^\nu) > U_1(\bar{x}^\mu,\bar{y}^\nu) \geq J_1(\mu,\nu),$$

$$J_2(\mu,\delta_{y^*}) = \int_{A_1} U_2(x,y^*)\mu(dx) = U_2(\bar{x}^\mu,y^*) > U_2(\bar{x}^\mu,\bar{y}^\nu) \geq J_2(\mu,\nu).$$

This is also true if (μ,ν) is in C_2. Hence, for any $\epsilon > 0$, the vector $\delta_{(x^*,y^*)} = (\delta_{x^*},\delta_{y^*})$ is a SUP in the set C. Therefore, by Theorem 21, for $\epsilon > 0$ the set $C \cap V_\epsilon(\delta_{(x^*,y^*)})$ is invariant for (47). Moreover, since, for every i in I, the payoff functions $U_i(\cdot)$ are continuous and the sets of strategies A_i are compact sets, we conclude by Theorem 21 and Remark 23 that if $\mu(0) \in C \cap V_\epsilon(\delta_{(x^*,y^*)})$, then $\mu(t) \to \delta_{(x^*,y^*)}$ in distribution.

3.6.2 The Tragedy of the Commons

In Section 2.3, we saw that there is a unique Nash equilibrium $(x_1^*,\ldots,x_n^*)$ for the "tragedy of the commons." We will prove that it is also a SUP for the game.

For each player i in I, we define the following sets:

$$H_i^1 := \{x_i \in A_i \colon x_i \leq x_i^*\}, \quad H_i^2 := \{x_i \in A_i \colon x_i \geq x_i^*\},$$
$$C_1 := \{(\mu_1,\ldots,\mu_n) \in \mathbb{P}(A_1)\times\cdots\times\mathbb{P}(A_n) \colon \mu_i(H_i^1) = 1 \quad \forall i \in I\},$$
$$C_2 := \{(\mu_1,\ldots,\mu_n) \in \mathbb{P}(A_1)\times\cdots\times\mathbb{P}(A_n) \colon \mu_i(H_i^2) = 1 \quad \forall i \in I\}.$$

Let $(x_1,\ldots,x_n)$ be a profile such that $x_i \leq x_i^*$ for all i in I with strict inequality for some player i. Let $\hat{x} := x_1 + \cdots + x_n$, and $\hat{x}^* := x_1^* + \cdots + x_j^* + \cdots + x_n^*$, so $\hat{x} < \hat{x}^*$.

For all i in I, let U_i be as in (29) and consider the left-hand side of (30). Since $v' < 0$ and $v'' < 0$, then we have $0 < v(\hat{x}^*) < v(\hat{x})$ and $v'(\hat{x}^*) < v'(\hat{x}) < 0$. Therefore, for each i in I

$$\frac{\partial U_i(x_i,x_{-i})}{\partial x_i} = v(\hat{x}) + x_i v'(\hat{x}) - c_i > v(\hat{x}^*) + x_i^* v'(\hat{x}^*) - c_i = 0.$$

Thus the map $x_i \mapsto U_i(x_i,x_{-i})$ is increasing in $[0,x_i^*]$, and

$$U_i(x_i^*,x_{-i}) > U_i(x_i,x_{-i}) \quad \forall x_i \in H_i^1,\ x_{-i} \in H_{-i}^1, \tag{81}$$

where $H^1_{-i} = H^1_1 \times \cdots \times H^1_{i-1} \times H^1_{i+1} \times \cdots \times H^1_n$.

Similarly, if $(x_1, \ldots, x_n)$ is a profile such that $x_i \geq x_i^*$ for all i in I with strict inequality for some player i, then the map $x_i \mapsto U_i(x_i, x_{-i})$ is decreasing in $[x_i^*, \bar{x}]$, where $\bar{x}$ is the maximum capacity of the network to transmit data in a given amount of time. Hence

$$U_i(x_i^*, x_{-i}) > U_i(x_i, x_{-i}) \quad \forall x_i \in H_i^2,\ x_{-i} \in H^2_{-i}, \tag{82}$$

where $H^2_{-i} = H^2_1 \times \cdots \times H^2_{i-1} \times H^2_{i+1} \times \cdots \times H^2_n$.

Let $C = C_1 \cup C_2$. If $\mu \in C$, then by (81) and (82)

$$J_i(\delta_{x^*}, \mu_{-i}) > J_i(\mu_i, \mu_{-i}) \quad \forall i \in I.$$

Hence, for any $\epsilon > 0$, the vector $\delta_{x^*} = (\delta_{x_1^*}, \ldots, \delta_{x_n^*})$ is a SUP in the set C. By Theorem 21, the set $C \cap V_\epsilon(\delta_{x^*})$ is invariant for (47). Moreover, since, for every i in I, the payoff functions $U_i(\cdot)$ are continuous and the sets of strategies A_i are compact sets, we conclude by Remark 23 that if $\mu(0) \in C \cap V_\epsilon(\delta_{x^*})$, then $\mu(t) \to \delta_{x^*}$ in distribution.

3.6.3 A Poverty Trap Model

In Section 2.4, we saw that there are three Nash equilibria for the game described by Table 1. We will prove that the pure Nash equibribria $\delta_{(s,m)} = (\delta_s, \delta_m)$ and $\delta_{(a,\tau)} = (\delta_a, \delta_\tau)$ are SUPs. To this end, consider the Nash equilibrium (μ^*, ν^*) described by (32) and (33), respectively.

Let $k_1 = \max\{\mu^*(s), \nu^*(m)\}$ and $k_2 = \max\{1 - \mu^*(s), 1 - \nu^*(m)\}$. Note that the sets of pure strategies for workers and firms are $A_w = \{s, a\}$ and $A_f = \{m, \tau\}$, respectively. Consider the sets

$$C_1 := \{(\mu, \nu) \in \mathbb{P}(A_w) \times \mathbb{P}(A_f) \colon k_1 < \mu(s), k_1 < \nu(m)\},$$
$$C_2 := \{(\mu, \nu) \in \mathbb{P}(A_w) \times \mathbb{P}(A_f) \colon k_2 < \mu(a), k_2 < \nu(\tau)\}.$$

It is easy to check that for any $(\mu, \nu) \in C_1$,

$$J_w(\delta_s, \nu) > J_w(\mu, \nu) \quad \text{and} \quad J_f(\mu, \delta_m) > J_f(\mu, \nu),$$

where J_w and J_f are the expected payoffs described by (18) of the workers and firms, respectively. Similarly, if $(\mu, \nu) \in C_2$, then

$$J_w(\delta_a, \nu) > J_w(\mu, \nu) \quad \text{and} \quad J_f(\mu, \delta_\tau) > J_f(\mu, \nu).$$

Let $\epsilon_1 = 1 - k_1$ and $\epsilon_2 = 1 - k_2$. Note that $\|\delta_w - \mu\| = 1 - \mu(w)$ and $\|\delta_f - \nu\| = 1 - \nu(f)$ for any $w \in A_w$ and $f \in A_f$. The open balls $V_{\epsilon_1}(\delta_{(s,m)})$ and $V_{\epsilon_2}(\delta_{(s,m)})$ (introduced in (68)) satisfy that $V_{\epsilon_1}(\delta_{(s,m)}) = C_1$ and $V_{\epsilon_2}(\delta_{(s,m)}) = C_2$. This proves that $\delta_{(s,m)}$ and $\delta_{(a,\tau)}$ are SUPs with barriers ϵ_1 and ϵ_2 respectively.

Hence, the conditions of Corollary 22 are satisfied, and so $\delta_{(s,m)}$ and $\delta_{(a,\tau)}$ are Lyapunov stable for the replicator dynamics. Moreover, since the action spaces A_w and A_f are finite sets, then the replicator dynamics are in $\mathbb{R}^n$ ($n = 4$ in this case), and the maps $(\mu_i, \mu_{-i}) \mapsto J_i(a_i, \mu_{-i}(t)) - J_i(\mu_i(t), \mu_{-i}(t))$ are continuous for $i = w, f$. Therefore, $\delta_{(s,m)}$ and $\delta_{(a,\tau)}$ are weakly attracting.

3.7 Comments

In this section, we introduced a model of asymmetric evolutionary games with strategies in metric spaces. The model can be reduced, of course, to the particular case of evolutionary games with finite strategy sets. We established conditions under which the replicator dynamics has a solution and we also characterized that solution (Theorem 13). Then stability conditions were established, and finally we gave three examples. The first one may be applicable to oligopoly models, theory of international trade, and public good models. The second and third examples deal with the tragedy of commons game and a model of poverty traps.

There are many questions, however, that remain open. For instance, in symmetric evolutionary games with continuous strategy spaces, there are stability conditions with different metrics and topologies. Are these conditions satisfied in the asymmetric case? Narang and Shaiju (2019, 2020, 2022) analyze, define new static equilibria, and establish conditions for the stability of the replicator dynamics in asymmetric games where special Nash equilibria are vectors of atomic probability measures. Are there conditions for the stability when the Nash equilibria are vectors of nonatomic measures? Mendoza-Palacios and Hernández-Lerma (2019) present a survey about stability for the replicator dynamics in symmetric and asymmetric games with strategies in metric spaces.

On the other hand, normal-form games with continuous strategies can be approximated by games with discrete strategies. Hence, it would be interesting to investigate if the replicator dynamics with continuous strategies in the asymmetric case can be approximated, in some sense, by games with discrete strategies; see Section 5.

4 Evolutionary Games: Symmetric Case

In Section 3.2.1 we saw how to obtain a symmetric evolutionary game (52) from an asymmetric one (49). In this section we provide a general framework to study the replicator dynamics for symmetric evolutionary games in which the strategy set is a separable metric space. In this case, the replicator dynamics evolve in a space of signed measures, which is well known (in particular, the space of probability measures). This allows us to study stability criteria with respect to different topologies and metrics on a space of probability measures, and to establish a relation between symmetric Nash equilibria (of a two-player normal-form game (24)) and the stability of the replicator dynamics in different metrics.

In a two-player normal-form game a symmetric Nash equilibrium can be expressed in terms of a NES (see Definition 7). Similarly, a symmetric SUP can be written in terms of a *strongly uninvadable strategy* (Definition 26). This fact allows us to obtain more stability criteria than in the asymmetric case.

This section is organized as follows. Section 4.1 describes the replicator dynamics and their relation to evolutionary games (compare with sections 3.1–3.2). Some important technical issues are also summarized. Section 4.2 establishes the relation between the replicator dynamics and a normal-form game using the concepts of *Nash equilibria* and *strongly uninvadable strategies*. Section 4.3 presents a brief review of results on the stability of the replicator dynamics. Different stability criteria with respect to various metrics and topologies are standardized in the sense that the results (see Theorem 33, Conjecture 34, and Remark 35) are expressed in terms of a suitable general metric on a space of probability measures. (For instance, in some cases the metric is required to metrize the weak topology.)

Section 4.4 establishes an important relationship between Nash equilibria and the critical points of the replicator dynamics (Theorem 38 and Remarks 39 and 40). Section 4.5 proposes examples to illustrate our results. Finally, we conclude in Section 4.6 with some general comments on possible extensions of our results.

In this section we use the technical preliminaries in Section 1, in particular, Section 1.3.2.

4.1 The Model

4.1.1 Symmetric Evolutionary Games

Consider a population of individuals of a single species. Each individual of this species can choose a single element a in a set of characteristics (the set of pure strategies or pure actions) A, which is a separable metric space. Let $\mathcal{B}(A)$ be the Borel σ-algebra of A, and $\mathbb{P}(A)$ the set of probability measures on A, also known as the set of mixed strategies.

Moreover, consider a payoff function $J\colon \mathbb{P}(A) \times \mathbb{P}(A) \to \mathbb{R}$ that explains the interrelation between the population, and which is defined as

$$J(\mu, \nu) := \int_A \int_A U(a, b)\nu(db)\mu(da), \tag{83}$$

where $U: A \times A \rightarrow \mathbb{R}$ is a given measurable function. If δ_a is a probability measure concentrated at $a \in A$, the vector (δ_a, μ) is written as (a, μ), and then

$$J(\delta_a, \mu) = J(a, \mu).$$

In particular, (83) yields

$$J(\mu, \nu) := \int_A J(a, \nu)\mu(da). \tag{84}$$

In an evolutionary game, the strategies' dynamics is determined by a differential equation of the form

$$\mu'(t) = F(\mu(t)) \quad t \geq 0, \tag{85}$$

with some initial condition $\mu(0) = \mu_0$. The notation $\mu'(t)$ represents the strong derivative of $\mu(t)$ (see Definition 5), and $F(\cdot)$ is a mapping $F: \mathbb{P}(A) \rightarrow \mathbb{M}(A)$. More explicitly we write (85) as

$$\mu'(t, E) = F(\mu(t), E) \quad \forall E \in \mathcal{B}(A), \tag{86}$$

where $\mu'(t, E)$ and $F(\mu(t), E)$ are the measures $\mu'(t)$ and $F(\mu(t))$ valued at $E \in \mathcal{B}(A)$.

We shall be working with a special class of symmetric evolutionary games that can be described as a quadruple (compare with (52))

$$\left[I,\ \mathbb{P}(A),\ J(\cdot),\ \mu'(t) = F(\mu(t))\right], \tag{87}$$

where

(i) $I = \{1,2\}$ is the set of players;

(ii) for each player $i = 1,2$ we have a set $\mathbb{P}(A)$ of mixed actions and a payoff function $J: \mathbb{P}(A) \times \mathbb{P}(A) \rightarrow \mathbb{R}$ (as in (83)); and

(iii) the dynamics (85) are described by the replicator equation in (51), that is, for each E in $\mathbb{B}(A)$,

$$F(\mu(t), E) := \int_E \left[J(a, \mu(t)) - J(\mu(t), \mu(t))\right] \mu(t, da). \tag{88}$$

To obtain a heuristic approach to the replicator dynamics (85), with $F(\cdot)$ as in (88), one can proceed, of course, as in Section 3.2.

4.1.2 Technical Issues on the Replicator Dynamics

For a better understanding of this section, Theorem 24 summarizes conditions for the existence of a unique solution to the differential equation (85) (with $F(\cdot)$ as in (88)), and important properties of this solution; see also Theorems 12 and 13.

For each $t \geq 0$, let

$$\beta(a|\mu(t)) := J(a, \mu(t)) - J(\mu(t), \mu(t)), \tag{89}$$

which is the integrand of (88). Hence, by (89), $\beta(\cdot|\mu(t))$ is the Radon–Nikodym density of $F(\mu(t))$ with respect to $\mu(t)$, that is,

$$F(\mu(t), E) = \int_E \beta(a|\mu(t))\mu(t, da) \quad \forall E \in \mathcal{B}(A).$$

Theorem 24 *Suppose that the function $\beta(\cdot|\mu)$ in (89) satisfies:*

(*i*) *there exists $C \geq 0$ such that*

$$|\beta(a|\mu)| \leq C \quad \forall a \in A \text{ and } \|\mu\| \leq 2,$$

(*ii*) *there is a constant $D > 0$ such that*

$$\sup_{a \in A} |\beta(a|\eta) - \beta(a|\nu)| \leq D\|\eta - \nu\| \quad \forall \nu, \eta \text{ with } \|\eta\|, \|\nu\| \leq 2.$$

Then there exists a unique solution to the replicator dynamics (85). *Moreover, if $\mu(t)$ is a solution of* (85) *with initial condition $\mu(0)$ in $\mathbb{P}(A)$, then $\mu(0) \ll \mu(t)$ and $\mu(t) \ll \mu(0)$ for all $t > 0$, with Radon–Nikodym density*

$$\frac{d\mu(t)}{d\mu(0)}(a) = e^{\int_0^t \beta(a|\mu(s))ds}. \tag{90}$$

In particular, for every $t > 0$, if ν is a probability measure satisfying that $\nu \ll \mu(t)$ whenever $\nu \ll \mu(0)$, then

$$\log \frac{d\nu}{d\mu(t)}(a) = \log \frac{d\nu}{d\mu(0)}(a) - \int_0^t \beta(a|\mu(s))ds. \tag{91}$$

4.2 The Replicator Dynamics, NESs and SUSs

In this section we consider symmetric evolutionary games as in (87) and compare them with two-player symmetric normal-form games (24). We wish to study the relation between a Nash equilibrium of a normal-form game and the replicator dynamics (Proposition 25). We also define the important concept of *strongly uninvadable strategy* (Definition 26) and analyze its relation to a Nash equilibrium (Proposition 29).

In the rest of the section, we consider the *two-player symmetric normal-form game* Γ_s in (24), and the concept of *Nash equilibrium strategy* (NES) in Definition 7.

Proposition 25 *Let μ^* be a* NES *for* Γ_s. *Then μ^* is a critical point of* (85) *(i.e., $F(\mu^*) = 0$) when $F(\cdot)$ is described by the replicator dynamics* (88).

Proof See Theorem 16. (See also Mendoza-Palacios and Hernández-Lerma (2015), theorem 5.4.) □

The following definition is a slightly modified version of the strongly uninvadable strategies used in Bomze (1991).

Definition 26 *Let r be a metric on $\mathbb{P}(A)$ as in Remark 2. A measure $\mu^* \in \mathbb{P}(A)$ is called an r-* strongly uninvadable strategy (r-SUS) *if there exists $\epsilon > 0$ such that for any μ with $r(\mu, \mu^*) < \epsilon$, it follows that $J(\mu^*, \mu) > J(\mu, \mu)$. We call ϵ the global invasion barrier.*

When r is the Prokhorov metric r_p, Oechssler and Riedel (2002) name a r_p-SUS as an *evolutionary robust strategy*. If r_{w^*} is any metric that metrizes the weak topology (recall Remark 2), Cressman and Hofbauer (2005) call a r_{w^*}-SUS a *locally superior strategy*.

We use the notation $\|\cdot\|$-SUS when the metric on $\mathbb{P}(A)$ is given by the total variation norm (1).

Proposition 27 *Let r_{w^*} be a distance that metrizes the weak convergence on $\mathbb{P}(A)$. If a measure $\mu^* \in \mathbb{P}(A)$ is r_{w^*}-SUS, then it is $\|\cdot\|$-SUS.*

Proof Let μ be in the open ball $V_\epsilon^{\|\cdot\|}(\mu^*)$ defined in (13). Then there is some open neighborhood $\mathcal{V}_\epsilon^{\mathcal{H}}(\mu^*)$ of the form (4) such that $\mu \in \mathcal{V}_\epsilon^{\mathcal{H}}(\mu^*)$ and, by Remark 3, there is some open ball $\mathcal{V}_\alpha^{r_{w^*}}(\mu^*)$ such that $\mu \in \mathcal{V}_\alpha^{r_{w^*}}(\mu^*)$. Thus the proposition follows. □

The next lemma is a key fact to provide a general framework to the different stability criteria.

Lemma 28 *Let r_{w^*} be a distance that metrizes the weak convergence on $\mathbb{P}(A)$. For every $\mu, \nu \in \mathbb{P}(A)$ and $\epsilon > 0$, there exist α and α' in* $(0, 1)$ *and $\eta, \gamma \in \mathbb{P}(A)$ such that*

(i) $r_{w^*}(\eta, \mu) < \epsilon$ *if* $\eta = \alpha\nu + (1-\alpha)\mu$,
(ii) $\|\gamma - \mu\| < \epsilon$ *if* $\gamma = \alpha'\nu + (1-\alpha')\mu$.

Proof Let α_n be a sequence in $(0, 1)$ such that $\alpha_n \to 0$, and let $\eta_n := \alpha_n\nu + (1-\alpha_n)\mu$. If $f \in \mathbb{C}_B(A)$, then

$$\lim_{n\to\infty} \int_A f(a)\eta_n(da) = \lim_{n\to\infty} \alpha_n \int_A f(a)\nu(da) + \lim_{n\to\infty}(1-\alpha_n) \int_A f(a)\mu(da)$$
$$= \int_A f(a)\mu(da).$$

Hence, by Propositions 1 and 2 in section 2 of the online appendix, part (*i*) follows.

On the other hand, let $0 < \alpha' < \frac{\epsilon}{\|\nu - \mu\|}$. Then

$$\|\gamma - \mu\| = \|\alpha'\nu + (1-\alpha')\mu - \mu\| = \alpha'\|\nu - \mu\| < \epsilon,$$

and (*ii*) holds. □

The following proposition shows that a strongly uninvadable strategy is also a Nash equilibrum strategy. In other words, the concept of SUS is a refinement of NES.

Proposition 29 *Let r be a metric on* $\mathbb{P}(A)$ *as in Remark 2. If* μ^* *is a r-SUS, then* μ^* *is a NES of* Γ_s.

Proof Suppose that μ^* is not a NES of Γ_s. Then there exists $\nu \in \mathbb{P}(A)$ such that

$$J(\nu, \mu^*) > J(\mu^*, \mu^*). \tag{92}$$

By Lemma 28, there exists $\eta := \alpha\nu + (1-\alpha)\mu^*$ for some $\alpha \in (0,1)$, with $r(\eta, \mu^*) < \epsilon$. Since μ^* is r-SUS, $J(\mu^*, \eta) > J(\eta, \eta)$ and so

$$\begin{aligned}\alpha J(\mu^*, \nu) + (1-\alpha)J(\mu^*, \mu^*) > {} & \alpha\alpha J(\nu, \nu) + (1-\alpha)\alpha J(\nu, \mu^*) \\ & + (1-\alpha)\alpha J(\mu^*, \nu) \\ & + (1-\alpha)(1-\alpha)J(\mu^*, \mu^*).\end{aligned}$$

Hence

$$\alpha J(\mu^*, \nu) + (1-\alpha)J(\mu^*, \mu^*) > \alpha J(\nu, \nu) + (1-\alpha)J(\nu, \mu^*). \tag{93}$$

If (92) is true, then there exists $\alpha > 0$ sufficiently small such that (93) is violated. Thus μ^* is a NES for Γ_s. □

Now, we define the following sets:

(*i*) $\mathcal{N} := \{\mu^* \in \mathbb{P}(A) : \mu^* \text{ is a NES of } \Gamma_s\}$,
$\mathcal{C} := \{\mu^* \in \mathbb{P}(A) : \mu^* \text{ is a critical point of (85)}\}$.

(*ii*) If r is a metric on $\mathbb{P}(A)$ as in Remark 2,

$$r\text{-}\mathcal{SUS} := \{\mu^* \in \mathbb{P}(A) : \mu^* \text{ is } r\text{-SUS}\}$$

We can summarize Propositions 25 and 29 as follows:

Corollary 30 *Let A be a separable metric space and assume the conditions* (*i*) *and* (*ii*) *of Theorem 24. If r is a metric on* $\mathbb{P}(A)$ *as in Remark 2, then we have*

$$r\text{-}\mathcal{SUS} \subset \mathcal{N} \subset \mathcal{C}.$$

An improvement of this result is presented in Section 4.4 (see Theorem 38).

4.3 Stability of SUSs

This section presents a review of results on the stability of a SUS in the replicator dynamics. These results include different stability criteria with respect to various metrics and topologies in the space of probability measures. For some references on the results of this section, see Bomze (1990) and Mendoza-Palacios and Hernández-Lerma (2017, 2019).

4.3.1 The Kullback–Leibler Distance

Assume that $\nu \ll \mu$. We define the cross entropy or Kullback–Leibler distance of ν with respect to μ as

$$K(\mu,\nu) := \int_A \log\left[\frac{d\nu}{d\mu}(a)\right]\nu(da). \tag{94}$$

From Jensen's inequality it follows that $0 \le K(\mu,\nu) \le \infty$ and $K(\mu,\nu) = 0$ if and only if $\mu = \nu$. The Kullback–Leibler distance is not a metric, since it is not symmetric, that is, $K(\mu,\nu) \neq K(\nu,\mu)$.

Given $\mu^* \in \mathbb{P}(A)$, $\epsilon > 0$, and a strictly increasing function $\varphi\colon [0,\infty) \to [0,\infty)$, we define the set

$$\mathcal{W}_{\varphi(\epsilon)}(\mu^*) := \left\{\mu \in \mathbb{P}(A)\colon K(\mu,\mu^*) < \varphi(\epsilon)\right\}. \tag{95}$$

Theorem 31 *Suppose that A is a separable metric space, and that the conditions (i) and (ii) of Remark 8 hold. Let μ^* be a $\|\cdot\|$-SUS with global invasion barrier $\epsilon > 0$, and $\mu(\cdot)$ the solution of the replicator dynamics. If $\mu(0) \in \mathcal{W}_{\varphi(\epsilon)}(\mu^*)$ with $\varphi(\epsilon) = \left[\frac{\epsilon}{2}\right]^2$, then:*

(*i*) *$\mu(t) \in \mathcal{W}_{\varphi(\epsilon)}(\mu^*)$ for all $t \ge 0$;*
(*ii*) *$\|\mu(t) - \mu^*\| < \epsilon$ for all $t \ge 0$;*
(*iii*) *for all $t \ge 0$, $\mu(t)$ is in some open ball $\mathcal{V}_\alpha^{r_{w^*}}(\mu^*)$ as in (13), where r_{w^*} is any distance that metrizes the weak topology.*
(*iv*) *Moreover, if A is compact and the map $\mu \to J(\mu^*,\mu) - J(\mu,\mu)$ is continuous in the weak topology, then $r_{w^*}(\mu(t),\mu^*) \to 0$ as $t \to \infty$.*
(*v*) *Furthermore, parts (i) to (iv) are also true* with the hypothesis that μ^* is r_{w^*}-SUS.

Proof Parts (i), (ii), and (iv) are proved in Bomze (1990)[1]. Part (iii) is a consequence of (ii) and Remark 3. Finally, (v) follows from Proposition 27. □

4.3.2 The L_1-Wasserstein Metric

The following theorem characterizes the stability of the replicator dynamics with respect to the L_1-Wasserstein metric r_w in (12). This distance metrizes the weak topology and has important relationships with other distances that also metrize the weak topology (see Proposition 2). Furthermore, the L_1-Wasserstein metric is closely related to the variation norm (1) and the Kullback–Leibler distance (94); see Propositions 3 and 4. The following two theorems give better approximations to parts (iii) and (iv) of Theorem 31.

Theorem 32 *Suppose that A is a compact Polish space (with diameter $C > 0$), and the conditions (i) and (ii) of Theorem 24 hold. Let μ^* be a r_W-SUS with global invasion barrier $\epsilon > 0$, and $\mu(\cdot)$ the solution of the replicator dynamics. If $\mu(0) \in \mathcal{W}_{\varphi'(\epsilon)}(\mu^*)$ with $\varphi'(\epsilon) = \left[\frac{\epsilon}{2C}\right]^2$, then*

- (i) *$\mu(t) \in \mathcal{W}_{\varphi'(\epsilon)}(\mu^*)$ for all $t \geq 0$;*
- (ii) *$\|\mu(t) - \mu^*\| < \frac{\epsilon}{C}$ for all $t \geq 0$;*
- (iii) *$r_W(\mu(t), \mu^*) < \epsilon$ for all $t \geq 0$.*
- (iv) *Moreover, if the map $\mu \longrightarrow J(\mu^*, \mu) - J(\mu, \mu)$ is continuous in the weak topology, then $r_W(\mu(t), \mu^*) \longrightarrow 0$.*
- (v) *Furthermore, parts (i) to (iv) are also true with the hypothesis* that μ^* is $\|\cdot\|$-SUS with barrier $\frac{\epsilon}{C}$.

Proof (i) If $\mu(0)$ is in $\mathcal{W}_{\varphi'(\epsilon)}(\mu^*)$, then by Theorem 24 we know that $\mu^* \ll \mu(t)$ and so $K(\mu(t), \mu^*)$ is well-defined for all $t \geq 0$. Using Theorem 24 and Fubini's theorem,

$$K(\mu(t), \mu^*) - K(\mu(0), \mu^*) = -\int_A \left[\int_0^t \beta(a|\mu(s))ds\right] \mu^*(da)$$
$$= -\int_0^t J(\mu^*, \mu(s)) - J(\mu(s), \mu(s))ds. \tag{96}$$

By the condition (ii) of Theorem 24 there exists $D > 0$ such that, for any $a \in A$ and $\mu, \eta \in \mathbb{P}(A)$,

$$|\beta(a|\eta) - \beta(a|\nu)| \leq D\|\eta - \nu\|.$$

[1] Bomze (1990) proves a more general case for part (iv), where any topology τ on $\mathbb{P}(A)$ is considered. He only requires that $\mathbb{P}(A)$ be a τ-compact set and the map $\mu \longrightarrow J(\mu^*, \mu) - J(\mu, \mu)$ be τ-continuous.

So,

$$\left|[J(\mu^*,\eta) - J(\eta,\eta)] - [J(\mu^*,\nu) - J(\nu,\nu)]\right| = \left|\int_A [\beta(a|\eta) - \beta(a|\nu)]\mu^*(da)\right| \le D\|\eta - \nu\|. \quad (97)$$

By (97) and since $\mu(s)$ is continuous in s, the map $s \to [J(\mu^*, \mu(s)) - J(\mu(s), \mu(s))]$ is continuous. Therefore, the time derivative of $K(\mu(t), \mu^*)$ exists and since μ^* is a r_w-SUS,

$$\frac{dK(\mu(t), \mu^*)}{dt} = -[J(\mu^*, \mu(t)) - J(\mu(t), \mu(t))] \le 0. \quad (98)$$

Hence $K(\mu(t), \mu^*)$ is nonincreasing in t, and (i) holds.

Proof of (ii), (iii). By Proposition 3 and (96),

$$r_w(\mu(t), \mu^*) \le C\|\mu(t) - \mu^*\| \le 2C[K(\mu(0), \mu^*)]^{\frac{1}{2}} < \epsilon. \quad (99)$$

Therefore (ii) and (iii) hold.

$iv)$ Since $K(\mu(t), \mu^*)$ is a nonincreasing function in t and, by (96), the map

$$t \to \int_0^t \left[J(\mu^*, \mu(s)) - J(\mu(s), \mu(s))\right] ds$$

is increasing and

$$\lim_{t\to\infty} \int_0^t \left[J(\mu^*, \mu(s)) - J(\mu(s), \mu(s))\right] ds < \infty.$$

Moreover, since the map $s \to [J(\mu^*, \mu(s)) - J(\mu(s), \mu(s))]$ is continuous, we have $\lim_{s\to\infty} [J(\mu^*, \mu(s)) - J(\mu(s), \mu(s))] = 0$.

Since A is compact, the space $\mathbb{P}(A)$ is compact in the weak topology (see Bobrowski (2005)), and the distance r_w metrizes this topology (Proposition 2). Suppose now that $\hat{\mu}$ is an accumulation point of the trajectory $\mu(\cdot)$. By (99), the r_w-distance from $\hat{\mu}$ to μ^* is at most ϵ, and since μ^* is r_w-SUS, $J(\mu^*, \hat{\mu}) > J(\hat{\mu}, \hat{\mu})$ if $\hat{\mu} \neq \mu^*$. By hypothesis, the map $\mu \to J(\mu^*, \mu) - J(\mu, \mu)$ is weakly continuous. If $\hat{\mu}$ is such that $J(\mu^*, \hat{\mu}) - J(\hat{\mu}, \hat{\mu}) = 0$, then $\hat{\mu} = \mu^*$, which proves that $r_w(\mu(t), \mu^*) \to 0$.

(v) Finally if μ^* is $\|\cdot\|$-SUS with barrier $\frac{\epsilon}{C}$ then, by (99), parts (i) to (iv) follow. □

4.3.3 Stability of a Pure-SUS

The next theorem characterizes the stability of the replicator dynamics for a SUS that is also a Dirac measure. Some parts of the theorem require the set of actions A to be Polish space, that is, a complete and separable metric space.

Theorem 33 *Let A be a separable metric space and suppose that the conditions (i) and (ii) of Theorem 24 hold. Let δ_{a^*} be a Dirac measure and r any metric on $\mathbb{P}(A)$ as in Remark 2. Let us suppose that δ_{a^*} is r-SUS, $\mu(\cdot)$ is a solution of the replicator dynamics, and $||\mu_0 - \delta_{a^*}|| < \epsilon$ for some small $\epsilon > 0$. Then*

(i) *$||\mu(t) - \delta_{a^*}|| < \epsilon$ for all $t \geq 0$;*
(ii) *for all $t \geq 0$, $\mu(t)$ is in some open ball $\mathcal{V}_\alpha^{r_{w^*}}(\mu^*)$ as in (13), where r_{w^*} is any distance that metrizes the weak topology;*
(iii) *if A is a compact Polish space (with diameter $C > 0$), then for all $t \geq 0$, $r_w(\mu(t), \delta_{a^*}) < C\epsilon$;*
(iv) *if A is a compact metric space (not necessarly a Polish space) and the map $\mu \longrightarrow J(\delta_{a^*}, \mu) - J(\mu, \mu)$ is continuous in the weak topology, then $r_{w^*}(\mu(t), \mu^*) \longrightarrow 0$, where r_{w^*} is any distance that metrizes the weak topology.*

Proof Parts (*i*) and (*iv*) follow from Theorem 21 and Corollary 22. (See also Mendoza-Palacios and Hernández-Lerma (2015) Theorem 6.2.) Part (*ii*) follows for Proposition 27. Finally, part (*iii*) follows from Proposition 2. □

Theorem 33 is also proved by Oechssler and Riedel (2001) with slight changes in the definition of || ||-SUS.

4.3.4 Related Stability Results

The following conjecture was proposed by Oechssler and Riedel (2002), when r_{w^*} is a distance that metrizes the weak topology.

Conjecture 34 *Let r be any metric on $\mathbb{P}(A)$ and r_{w^*} any distance that metrizes the weak topology. Suppose that A is a separable metric space, and that the conditions (i) and (ii) of Theorem 24 hold. Let μ^* be a r-SUS and $\mu(\cdot)$ the solution of the replicator dynamics. Then*

(i) *for $\epsilon > 0$ there exist $\delta > 0$ such that if $r(\mu(0), \mu^*) < \delta$, we have that $r(\mu(t), \mu^*) < \epsilon$ for all $t \geq 0$;*
(ii) *moreover, if part (i) is satisfied, and the map $\mu \longrightarrow J(\mu^*, \mu) - J(\mu, \mu)$ is continuous in the weak topology and $\mu^* \ll \mu(0)$, then $r_{w^*}(\mu(t), \mu^*) \longrightarrow 0$.*

Remark 35 *A double symmetric game (named a potential game by Cressman and Hofbauer (2005)) is a game where $J(\mu, \nu) = J(\nu, \mu)$ for any $\mu, \nu \in \mathbb{P}(A)$. Let r_{w^*} be any distance that metrizes the weak topology. Oechssler and Riedel (2002) prove that if A is a compact set and μ^* is r_{w^*}- SUS, then for double symmetric games, μ^* satisfies part (i) of Conjecture 34. Cressman and Hofbauer*

(2005) prove that if part (i) is satisfied, then (ii) follows for any symmetric game.

Oechssler and Riedel (2002) prove that a r_{w^*}-*SUS* satisfies other static evolutionary concepts such as *evolutionary stable strategy* (ESS), *continuously stable strategy* (CSS), and *neighborhood invader strategy* (NIS), which characterize dynamic stability in the weak topology for the replicator dynamics. Eshel and Sansone (2003), Cressman (2005), and Cressman et al. (2006) use these evolutionary concepts and different hypotheses on the payoff function (83) to guarantee dynamic stability. Norman (2008) establishes the dynamic stability in terms of strategy sets.

4.4 NESs and Stability

In this section we introduce a general definition of dynamic stability for the replicator dynamics (see Definition 36), and prove that any *stable* critical point of the replicator dynamics is a NES of Γ_s (see Proposition 37). Moreover, in Theorem 38 and Remarks 39 and 40 we relate the stability of the differential equation (85), and the static evolutionary concepts NES and SUS.

Consider $\mu, \nu \in \mathbb{P}(A)$. By Propositions 2, 3, and 4 in section 2 of the online appendix, we know that if μ and ν are close with respect to the Kullback–Leibler distance K, then they are close in the total variation norm $\|\cdot\|$, and consequently they are close in the weak topology. This argument is not true in the opposite direction. Hence we say that the Kullback–Leibler distance is "stronger than" the total variation norm, and the total variation norm is "stronger than" any distance that metrizes the weak topology. Some of the results in this section can be seen in Mendoza-Palacios and Hernández-Lerma (2017, 2019).

Definition 36 *Let A be a separable metric space, and r_1 and r_2 the Kullback–Leibler distance or some metric in $\mathbb{P}(A)$ where r_1 is equal to or "stronger than" r_2. A critical point μ^* of the replicator dynamics* (85) *is said to be*

(*i*) $[r_1, r_2]$-stable (in symbols: $[r_1, r_2]$-S) *if, for any $\epsilon > 0$, there exists $\delta > 0$ such that if $r_1(\mu(0), \mu^*) < \delta$, then $r_2(\mu(t), \mu^*) < \epsilon$ for all $t > 0$. If $r_1 = r_2 = r^*$, then we only say that μ^** is r^*-stable (in symbols: r^*-S).

(*ii*) $[r_1, r_2]$-asymptotically weakly stable *if it is* $[r_1, r_2]$-stable *and* $\lim_{t\to\infty} \mu(t) = \mu^*$ *in the weak topology.*

Consider the Kullback–Leibler distance K, the total variation norm $\|\cdot\|$, and any distance r_{w^*} that metrizes the weak topology. The following diagram gives the natural implications between the different concepts of stability.

$$\begin{array}{ccccc} K\text{-S} & \Rightarrow & [K, \|\cdot\|]\text{-S} & \Rightarrow & [K, r_{w^*}]\text{-S} \\ & & \Uparrow & & \Uparrow \\ & & \|\cdot\|\text{-S} & \Rightarrow & [\|\cdot\|, r_{w^*}]\text{-S} \\ & & & & \Uparrow \\ & & & & r_{w^*}\text{-S} \end{array} \tag{100}$$

These implications are easy to deduce. For example, if the critical point μ^* is $\|\cdot\|$-S, and the initial condition μ_0 satisfies that $K(\mu_0, \mu^*) < \left(\frac{\epsilon}{2}\right)^2$ for a small $\epsilon > 0$, then by Proposition 3 $\|\mu_0 - \mu^*\| < \epsilon$, hence μ^* is also $[K, \|\cdot\|]$-S. On the other hand, μ^* is $\|\cdot\|$-S, and the initial condition μ_0 is such that $\|\mu(t) - \mu^*\| < \delta$ for all $t > 0$ and some $\delta > 0$, then by Remark 3 for any r_{w^*}-metric, $\mu(t) \in \mathcal{V}_\alpha^{r_{w^*}}$ for some small $\alpha > 0$. Hence μ^* is also $[\|\cdot\|, r_{w^*}]$-S.

Van Veelen and Spreij (2009) study other relationships among the different concepts of stability in diagram (100). They also study relationships between static evolutionary concepts and asymptotic evolutionary stability.

The proof of the following proposition uses *the support of a probability measure*; see Proposition 14.

Proposition 37 *Let A be a separable metric space, and r_1, r_2 the Kullback–Leibler distance or some metric in $\mathbb{P}(A)$ where r_1 is equal to or "stronger than" r_2. Suppose that the conditions (i) and (ii) of Theorem 24 are satisfied, and let μ^* be a critical point of* (85) *with $F(\cdot)$ as* (88). *If μ^* is $[r_1, r_2]$-stable, then μ^* is a Nash equilibrium strategy (NES) of Γ_s.*

Proof If μ^* is a critical point of (85) with $F(\cdot)$ as (88), then

$$J(a, \mu^*) - J(\mu^*, \mu^*) = 0 \quad \mu^*\text{-a.s.}$$

Suppose that μ^* is not a NES of Γ_s. Then there exist a' in A such that a' is not in the support of μ^* and

$$J(a', \mu^*) - J(\mu^*, \mu^*) > \kappa > 0 \tag{101}$$

for some κ. By the condition (ii) of Theorem 24 we have that for any $\mu, \eta \in \mathbb{P}(A)$

$$|\beta(a'|\eta) - \beta(a'|\nu)| \leq D\|\eta - \nu\|,$$

and so the map $\mu \to J(a', \mu) - J(\mu, \mu)$ is continuous. Hence, by (101), for any $\mu \in \mathbb{P}(A)$ near μ^* in some r_1 distance

$$J(a', \mu) - J(\mu, \mu) > \kappa. \tag{102}$$

Let $\epsilon > 0$ and $\mu_0 := \lambda_\epsilon \delta_{a'} + (1 - \lambda_\epsilon)\mu^*$ be the initial condition, where $\lambda_\epsilon \in (0, 1)$ and $\mu_0 \in \mathcal{W}_{\varphi(\epsilon)}(\mu^*)$ with $\varphi(\epsilon) = \epsilon^2$. The number λ_ϵ indeed exists since

$$K(\mu_0, \mu^*) = \int_{\text{Supp}(\mu^*)} \log\left[\frac{d\mu^*}{d\mu_0}(a)\right] \mu^*(da) = \log\left(\frac{1}{1 - \lambda_\epsilon}\right),$$

and the logarithmic function is continuous, and by Propositions 3 and 4, μ_0 is near μ^* in the r_1-distance.

By (102) and Theorem 24 we have

$$\mu(0,\{a'\})e^{\kappa t} \leq \mu(0,\{a'\})e^{\int_0^t \beta(a'|\mu(s))ds} = \mu(t,\{a'\}),$$

for all $t > 0$. Thus $\mu(t,\{a'\})$ is increasing if the initial condition is μ_0 and the trajectory $\mu(t)$ is not close to μ^* in the r_2-distance. So μ^* is not $[r_1,r_2]$-stable. □

Now, let r_1 and r_2 be the Kullback–Leibler distance or some metric on $\mathbb{P}(A)$, where r_1 is equal to or "stronger than" r_2. We define the following set:

$$[r_1,r_2]\text{-}\mathcal{S} := \{\mu^* \in \mathbb{P}(A) : \mu^* \text{ is } [r_1,r_2]\text{-S}\}.$$

Theorem 38 *Let A be a separable metric space, and consider the conditions (i) and (ii) of Theorem 24. Let r_1 be a metric on $\mathbb{P}(A)$, and let r_2 be the Kullback–Leibler distance or some metric on $\mathbb{P}(A)$ equal to or "stronger than" r_1. Consider the sets r_1-$\mathcal{SUS}$, $\mathcal{N}$ and $\mathcal{C}$ as in Corollary 30. Then we have:*

$$r_1\text{-}\mathcal{SUS} \subset [K,r_2]\text{-}\mathcal{S} \subset \mathcal{N} \subset \mathcal{C}.$$

Proof This is a consequence of Theorem 31 and Propositions 25 and 37. □

Remark 39 *Suppose the hypotheses of Theorem 38 and let A be a compact Polish space. Then by Theorem 32 and Propositions 2 and 3, we can obtain the implications in Theorem 38 with a specific value for the barrier $\epsilon > 0$, for the metrics $\|\cdot\|$, r_p, r_{bl}, r_w, r_{kr}.*

Remark 40 *Let r_1 and r_2 be the total variation norm* (1) *or some metric that metrizes the weak topology on $\mathbb{P}(A)$. By Theorem 33 and Propositions 25, 37, we have the following implications if a Dirac measure δ_{a^*} is a r_1-SUS.*

$$\delta_{a^*} \in r_1\text{-}\mathcal{SUS} \Rightarrow \delta_{a^*} \in [\|\ \|,r_2]\text{-}\mathcal{S} \Rightarrow \delta_{a^*} \in \mathcal{N} \Rightarrow \delta_{a^*} \in \mathcal{C}.$$

4.5 Examples

In this section we consider the examples in Sections 2.2, 2.6, and 2.7. In each example we prove that the NES of the game is also a SUS. Thus, under the replicator dynamics if the initial strategy μ_0 is close to the NES (which is a SUS), then the player selects a strategy $\mu(t)$ very close to the NES for every $t > 0$. In other words, under the replicator dynamics the player is searching and selecting strategies that have certain dominance, such as the SUSs.

4.5.1 A Linear-Quadratic Model

In this section we consider the symmetric form of the game in Section 2.2. Thus, we can rewrite the payoff functions (26) and (27) as

$$U(x,y) = -ax^2 - bxy + cx + dy,$$

with $a, b, c > 0$ and d any real number.

Let $A = [0, M]$, for $M > 0$, be the strategy set. If $2c(a-b) > 0$ and $4a^2 - b^2 > 0$, then we have an interior NES

$$x^* = \frac{2c(a-b)}{4a^2 - b^2}.$$

For a fixed y the function $U(x,y)$ is concave in x and has the partial derivative $U_x(x,y) = -2ax - by + c$. Let $x(y) := \text{argmax}\,U(x,y) = \frac{(c-by)}{2a}$ and note that $x'(y) = -(b/2a) < 0$. Then if $y < x^*$ or $x^* < y$,

$$U(x(y),y) > U(x^*,y) \geq U(y,y).$$

On the other hand, let $\bar{y}^\mu := \int_A y\mu(dy)$. If μ is such that $\bar{y}^\mu < x^*$, then by Jensen's inequality

$$J(\delta_{x^*}, \mu) = \int_{A_2} U(x^*,y)\mu(dy) = U(x^*,\bar{y}^\mu) > U(\bar{y}^\mu,\bar{y}^\mu) \geq J(\mu,\mu).$$

This is also true if $\bar{y}^\mu > x^*$. Hence, for any metric r on $\mathbb{P}(A)$, the strategy δ_{x^*} is r-SUS. Therefore, by Theorem 33, if $\|\mu_0 - \delta_{x^*}\| = 2(1 - \mu_0(\{x^*\})) < \epsilon$, then

$$\|\mu(t) - \delta_{x^*}\| = 2(1 - \mu(t,\{x^*\})) < \epsilon, \quad r_w(\mu(t), \delta_{x^*}) < M\epsilon \quad \forall t \geq 0.$$

Moreover, since the payoff function $U(\cdot)$ is continuous and the set A of strategies is compact, we conclude that $\mu(t) \to \delta_{x^*}$ in distribution.

4.5.2 Graduated Risk Game

Consider the game in Section 2.6. Theorems 6–10, 13 and page 120 in Bishop and Cannings (1978) show that if $v < c$ in the payoff function (37), then

$$U(x,y) = \begin{cases} vy + \frac{v-c}{2}(1-y) & \text{if } y > x, \\ \frac{v-c}{2}(1-x) & \text{if } y \leq x. \end{cases}$$

Hence the NES (38),

$$\frac{d\mu^*(x)}{dx} = \frac{\alpha - 1}{2} x^{\frac{\alpha-3}{2}},$$

satisfies that

$$J(\mu^*, \mu) - J(\mu, \mu) > 0 \quad \forall \mu \in \mathbb{P}(A),$$

that is, μ^* is a r-SUS for any metric r in $\mathbb{P}(A)$, with $A = [0, 1]$.

Hence, by Theorem 32, if $K(\mu_0, \mu^*) < \varphi'(\epsilon) = \left(\frac{\epsilon}{2}\right)^2$, then

(*i*) $\mu(t) \in \mathcal{W}_{\varphi'(\epsilon)}(\mu^*)$ for all $t \geq 0$;
(*ii*) $||\mu(t) - \mu^*|| < \epsilon$ for all $t \geq 0$;
(*iii*) $r_w(\mu(t), \mu^*) < \epsilon$ for all $t \geq 0$.

4.5.3 War of Attrition Game

Consider the game in Section 2.7. Theorems 6–11 in Bishop and Cannings (1978) show that if $v \leq m$ in the payoff function (40), then

$$U(x,y) = \begin{cases} v - y & \text{if } y < x, \\ \frac{v}{2} - y & \text{if } y = x, \\ -x & \text{if } y > x, \end{cases}$$

and the NES (41),

$$\frac{d\mu^*(x)}{dx} = \begin{cases} \frac{1}{v}e^{-x/v} & \text{if } x \in \left[0, m - \frac{v}{2}\right], \\ 0 & \text{if } x \in \left(m - \frac{v}{2}, m\right), \\ \text{a weight } \delta_m \cdot e^{1/2 - m/v} & \text{at the atom } \{m\}, \end{cases}$$

are such that

$$J(\mu^*, \mu) - J(\mu, \mu) > 0 \quad \forall \mu \in \mathbb{P}(A).$$

Hence μ^* is a r-SUS for any metric r in $\mathbb{P}(A)$, with $A = [0, m]$. Therefore, by Theorem 32, if $K(\mu_0, \mu^*) < \varphi'(\epsilon) = \left(\frac{\epsilon}{2m}\right)^2$ then

(*i*) $\mu(t) \in \mathcal{W}_{\varphi'(\epsilon)}(\mu^*)$ for all $t \geq 0$;
(*ii*) $||\mu(t) - \mu^*|| < \frac{\epsilon}{m}$ for all $t \geq 0$;
(*iii*) $r_w(\mu(t), \mu^*) < \epsilon$ for all $t \geq 0$.

4.6 Comments

In this section, we introduced a model of symmetric evolutionary games with strategies in measurable spaces. The model can be reduced, of course, to the particular case of evolutionary games with finite strategy sets. We provided a general framework to the replicator dynamics that allows us to analyze different stability criteria and also presented three examples. The first one may be applicable to oligopoly models, theory of international trade, and public good models. The second and third examples deal with a graduated risk game and a war of attrition game, respectively.

The replicator dynamics has been studied in other general spaces without direct applications to game theory. For instance, Kravvaritis et al. (2008, 2010, 2011); Kravvaritis and Papanicolaou (2011), and Papanicolaou and Smyrlis (2009) studied conditions for stability and examples for these general cases. These extensions may be applicable in areas such as migration, regional sciences, and spatial economics (see Fujita et al. (2001), chapters 5 and 6); or in industrial policy and innovation economics and development (see Almudi and Fatas-Villafranca (2021), Almudi et al. (2020a), Mendoza-Palacios et al. (2022), Mendoza-Palacios and Mercado (2021)).

There are still, however, many open issues. For instance, when the set of pure strategies is finite, Cressman (1997) shows that under some conditions the stability of monotone selection dynamics is locally determined by the replicator dynamics. Is this true for games with strategies in the space $\mathbb{P}(A)$ of probability measures? Another important issue would be to obtain a stability theorem for several evolutionary dynamics of games with continuous strategies similar to the result by Hofbauer and Sigmund (2003) (theorem 14) for games with a finite strategy set A.

5 Finite-Dimensional Approximations

In Sections 3 and 4 we see that for games with strategies in metric spaces, the replicator dynamics live in a space of measures. In this section we approximate this replicator dynamics (on infinite-dimensional spaces) by a sequence of dynamical systems on finite-dimensional spaces. Oechssler and Riedel (2002) propose two approximation theorems. The first one establishes the proximity of two paths generated by two different dynamical systems (the original model and a discrete approximation of the model) with the same initial condition. The second theorem establishes the proximity of two paths, each with different initial conditions, and these paths satisfy the same differential equation (85) with $F(\cdot)$ as (88).

In our development, there are two approximation results with hypotheses less restrictive than those by Oechssler and Riedel (2002) and extend their results. First, in our case, the approximation theorems are for symmetric and asymmetric games. Second, our two theorems provide conditions for the proximity of two paths generated by two different dynamical systems (the original model and a discrete approximation model) with different initial conditions. Moreover, our approximation results are presented using the total variational norm, for conditions studied in the strong topology, and also using the Kantorovich–Rubinstein metric, for conditions in the weak topology. Some of the results of this section can be seen in Mendoza-Palacios and Hernández-Lerma (2020).

This section is organized as follows. Section 5.1 presents a finite-dimensional technique for the approximation of static games in metric spaces; also, it proposes a finite-dimensional dynamical system to approximate the replicator dynamics in a Banach space. Sections 5.2 and 5.3 present approximation theorems for the replicator dynamics on measurable spaces by means of a finite-dimensional dynamical system (which may be the one proposed in Section 5.1). In Section 5.2 we use the total variation norm for the approximation, and in Section 5.3 we use the Kantorovich–Rubinstein metric. Section 5.4 proposes examples to illustrate our results. Finally, we conclude in section 5.5 with some general comments.

5.1 Discrete Approximations to the Replicator Dynamics

In order to obtain a finite-dimensional approximation of the replicator dynamics (46)–(47) (with $F_i(\cdot)$ as in (50)), for an asymmetric (49) (or symmetric (52)–(87)) game, we can apply Theorems 43 and 50 to a discrete approximation of the payoff functions U_i in (18) and the initial probability measures $\mu_{i,0}$, for i in I. For some approximation techniques for the payoff function in games, see Bishop and Cannings (1978), Simon (1987).

5.1.1 Games with Strategies in Intervals

Following Oechssler and Riedel (2002) (who propose a finite approximation for a symmetric game), consider an asymmetric game (49) where, for every i in I, $A_i = [c_{i,1}, c_{i,2}]$ (for some real numbers $c_{i,1} < c_{i,2}$), and U_i (as in (18)) is a real-valued bounded function. For every i in I, consider the partition $P_{i,k_i} := \{\xi_{i,m}\}_{m=0}^{2^{k_i}-1}$ over A_i, where

$$\xi_{i,m} := [a_{i,m}, a_{i,m+1}), \quad a_{i,m} = c_{i,1} + \frac{m[c_{i,2} - c_{i,1}]}{2^{k_i}},$$

for $m = 0, 1, \ldots, 2^{k_i} - 1$ and $\xi_{i,2^{k_i}-1} := [a_{i,2^{k_i}-1}, c_{i,2}]$. For every i in I, the discrete approximation to U_i is given by the function

$$U_{k_i}(x_1, \ldots, x_i, \ldots, x_n) := U_i(a_{1,m}, \ldots, a_{i,m'}, \ldots, a_{n,m''}),$$

if $(x_1, \ldots, x_i, \ldots, x_n)$ is in $\xi_{1,m} \times \cdots \times \xi_{i,m'} \times \cdots \times \xi_{n,m''}$. Also, for each i in I we approximate a probability measure $\mu_i \in \mathbb{P}(A_i)$ by a discrete probability distribution μ_{k_i} on the partition set P_{i,k_i}. Then we can write the approximation to the payoff function (18) as

$$J_{k_i}(\mu_{k_1}, \ldots, \mu_{k_n}) := \sum_{\xi_{1,m} \in P_{1,k_1}} \cdots \sum_{\xi_{n,m'} \in P_{n,k_n}} U_i(a_{1,m}, \ldots, a_{n,m'}) \mu_{k_n}(\xi_{n,m'}) \cdots \mu_{k_1}(\xi_{1,m}). \tag{103}$$

For every $i \in I$ and every vector $\mu_k := (\mu_{k_1}, \ldots, \mu_{k_n})$ in

$$\mathbb{P}(P_{1,k_1}) \times \cdots \times \mathbb{P}(P_{n,k_n}),$$

we write μ_k as (μ_{k_i}, μ_{-k_i}), where $\mu_{-k_i} := (\mu_{k_1}, \ldots, \mu_{k_{i-1}}, \mu_{k_{i+1}}, \ldots, \mu_{k_n})$ is in

$$\mathbb{P}(P_{1,k_1}) \times \cdots \times \mathbb{P}(P_{i-1,k_{i-1}}) \times \mathbb{P}(P_{i+1,k_{i+1}}) \times \cdots \times \mathbb{P}(P_{n,k_n}).$$

If $\delta_{\{\xi_{i,m}\}}$ is a probability measure concentrated at $\xi_{i,m} \in P_{i,k_i}$, the vector $(\delta_{\{\xi_{i,m}\}}, \mu_{-k_i})$ is written as $(a_{i,m}, \mu_{-k_i})$, and so

$$J_{k_i}(\delta_{\{\xi_{i,m}\}}, \mu_{-k_i}) = J_{k_i}(a_{i,m}, \mu_{-k_i}). \tag{104}$$

In particular, (103) yields

$$J_{k_i}(\mu_{k_i}, \mu_{-k_i}) := \sum_{\xi_{i,m} \in P_{i,k_i}} J_{k_i}(a_{i,m}, \mu_{-k_i}) \mu_{k_i}(\xi_{i,m}). \tag{105}$$

Note that $\mu_k := (\mu_{k_1}, \ldots, \mu_{k_n})$ in $\mathbb{P}(P_{1,k_1}) \times \cdots \times \mathbb{P}(P_{n,k_n})$ is a vector of measures in $\mathbb{P}(A_1) \times \cdots \times \mathbb{P}(A_n)$. Then for any $i \in I$ and $E_i \in \mathcal{B}(A_i) \cap P_{i,k_i}$, the replicator induced by $\{U_{k_i}\}_{i \in I}$ has the form,

$$\mu'_{k_i}(t, E_i) = \sum_{\xi_{i,m_i} \in E_i \cap P_{i,k_i}} \Big[J_{k_i}(a_{i,m}, \mu_{-k_i}(t)) - J_{k_i}(\mu_{k_i}(t), \mu_{-k_i}(t)) \Big] \mu_{k_i}(t, \xi_{i,m}), \tag{106}$$

which is equivalent to the system of differential equations in $\mathbb{R}^{2^{k_1} + \cdots + 2^{k_n}}$ of the form

$$\mu'_{k_i}(t, \xi_{i,m}) = \Big[J_{k_i}(a_{i,m}, \mu_{-k_i}(t)) - J_{k_i}(\mu_{k_i}(t), \mu_{-k_i}(t)) \Big] \mu_{k_i}(t, \xi_{i,m}), \tag{107}$$

for $i = 1, 2, \ldots, n$ and $m = 0, 1, \ldots, 2^{k_i} - 1$, with initial condition $\{\mu_{k_i,0}(\xi_{i,m})\}_{m=0}^{2^{k_i}-1}$.

Hence, using Theorem 43 or Theorem 50, we can approximate (46)–(47), with $F_i(\cdot)$ as in (50), by a system of differential equations in $\mathbb{R}^{2^{k_1} + \cdots + 2^{k_n}}$ of the form (107); see Remarks 46 and 52.

5.1.2 Games with Strategies in Compact Metric Spaces

As in Section 5.1.1, consider an asymmetric game (49) where, for every i in I, A_i is a compact metric space, and U_i (as in (18)) is a real-valued bounded function.

For every i in I, consider the partition $P_{i,k_i} := \{A_{i,m}\}_{m=0}^{2^{k_i}-1}$ over A_i, where $m = 0, 1, \ldots, 2^{k_i} - 1$. For any i in I and a fixed profile $(a_{1,m}, \ldots, a_{i,m'}, \ldots, a_{n,m''}) \in A_{1,m} \times \cdots \times A_{i,m'} \times \cdots \times A_{n,m''}$ the discrete approximation to U_i is given by the function

$$U_{k_i}(x_1, \ldots, x_i, \ldots, x_n) := U_i(a_{1,m}, \ldots, a_{i,m'}, \ldots, a_{n,m''}),$$

if $(x_1, \ldots, x_i, \ldots, x_n)$ is in $A_{1,m} \times \cdots \times A_{i,m'} \times \cdots \times A_{n,m''}$. Let us suppose that for each i in I we can approximate a probability measure $\mu_i \in \mathbb{P}(A_i)$ by a discrete probability distribution μ_{k_i} on the partition set P_{i,k_i}. Then we can write the approximation to the payoff function (18) as

$$J_{k_i}(\mu_{k_1}, \ldots, \mu_{k_n}) := \sum_{A_{1,m} \in P_{1,k_1}} \cdots \sum_{A_{n,m'} \in P_{n,k_n}} U_i(a_{1,m}, \ldots, a_{n,m'}) \mu_{k_n}(A_{n,m'}) \cdots \mu_{k_1}(A_{1,m}). \tag{108}$$

For every $i \in I$ and every vector $\mu_k := (\mu_{k_1}, \ldots, \mu_{k_n})$ in

$$\mathbb{P}(P_{1,k_1}) \times \cdots \times \mathbb{P}(P_{n,k_n}),$$

we write μ_k as (μ_{k_i}, μ_{-k_i}), where $\mu_{-k_i} := (\mu_{k_1}, \ldots, \mu_{k_{i-1}}, \mu_{k_{i+1}}, \ldots, \mu_{k_n})$ is in

$$\mathbb{P}(P_{1,k_1}) \times \cdots \times \mathbb{P}(P_{i-1,k_{i-1}}) \times \mathbb{P}(P_{i+1,k_{i+1}}) \times \cdots \times \mathbb{P}(P_{n,k_n}).$$

Note that $\mu_k := (\mu_{k_1}, \ldots, \mu_{k_n})$ in $\mathbb{P}(P_{1,k_1}) \times \cdots \times \mathbb{P}(P_{n,k_n})$ is a vector of measures in $\mathbb{P}(A_1) \times \cdots \times \mathbb{P}(A_n)$. Then for any $i \in I$ and $E_i \in \mathcal{B}(A_i) \cap P_{i,k_i}$, the replicator induced by $\{U_{k_i}\}_{i \in I}$ has the form

$$\mu'_{k_i}(t, E_i) = \sum_{A_{i,m} \in E_i \cap P_{i,k_i}} \left[J_{k_i}(a_{i,m}, \mu_{-k_i}(t)) - J_{k_i}(\mu_{k_i}(t), \mu_{-k_i}(t)) \right] \mu_{k_i}(t, A_{i,m}), \tag{109}$$

which is equivalent to the system of differential equations in $\mathbb{R}^{2^{k_1} + \cdots + 2^{k_n}}$ of the form:

$$\mu'_{k_i}(t, A_{i,m}) = \left[J_{k_i}(a_{i,m}, \mu_{-k_i}(t)) - J_{k_i}(\mu_{k_i}(t), \mu_{-k_i}(t)) \right] \mu_{k_i}(t, A_{i,m}), \tag{110}$$

for $i = 1, 2, \ldots, n$ and $m = 0, 1, \ldots, 2^{k_i} - 1$, with initial condition $\{\mu_{k_i,0}(A_{i,m})\}_{m=0}^{2^{k_i}-1}$.

As in Section 5.1.1, using Theorem 43 or Theorem 50, we can approximate (46)–(47), with $F_i(\cdot)$ as in (50), by a system of differential equations in $\mathbb{R}^{2^{k_1} + \cdots + 2^{k_n}}$; see Remarks 46 and 52.

5.2 An Approximation Theorem in the Strong Form

In this section we provide an approximation theorem that gives conditions under which we can approximate (46)–(47) (with $F_i(\cdot)$ as in (50)) by a finite-dimensional dynamical system of the form (107) under the total variation norm (1)

The proof of this theorem uses the following two lemmas, which are proved in the online appendix.

Lemma 41 *For each i in I, let A_i be a separable metric space. If each map $\mu_i\colon [0,\infty) \to \mathbb{M}(A_i)$ is* strongly differentiable, *then*

$$\frac{d\|\mu(t)\|_\infty}{dt} \leq \|\mu'(t)\|_\infty.$$

Proof See Section 3.1 of the online appendix. □

Lemma 42 *For each i in I, let A_i be a separable metric space and let $F(\cdot)$ be as in* (46)–(47) *(with $F_i(\cdot)$ as in* (50)*). Suppose that for each i in I the payoff function $U_i(\cdot)$ in* (18) *is bounded. Then*

$$\|F(\nu) - F(\mu)\|_\infty \leq Q\|\nu - \mu\|_\infty \quad \forall \mu, \nu \in \mathbb{P}(A_1) \times \cdots \times \mathbb{P}(A_n), \tag{111}$$

where $Q := (2n+1)H$ and $H := \max_{i\in I} \|U_i\|$.

Proof See Section 3.2 of the online appendix. □

Theorem 43 *For each i in I, let A_i be a separable metric space and let $U_i, U_i^\epsilon : A_1 \times \cdots \times A_n \to \mathbb{R}$ be bounded functions such that $\max_{i\in I} \|U_i - U_i^\epsilon\| < \epsilon$, where $\|\cdot\|$ is the sup norm in* (2)*. Consider the replicator dynamics induced by $\{U_i\}_{i=1}^n$ and $\{U_i^\epsilon\}_{i=1}^n$, that is,*

$$\mu_i'(t, E_i) = \int_{E_i} \Big[J_i(a_i, \mu_{-i}(t)) - J_i(\mu_i(t), \mu_{-i}(t))\Big]\mu_i(t, da_i), \tag{112}$$

$$\nu_i'(t, E_i) = \int_{E_i} \Big[J_i^\epsilon(a_i, \nu_{-i}(t)) - J_i^\epsilon(\nu_i(t), \nu_{-i}(t))\Big]\nu_i(t, da_i), \tag{113}$$

for each $i \in I$, $E_i \in \mathcal{B}(A_i)$, and $t \geq 0$. If $\mu(\cdot)$ and $\nu(\cdot)$ are solutions of (112) *and* (113)*, respectively, with initial conditions $\mu(0) = \mu_0$ and $\nu(0) = \nu_0$, then for $T < \infty$*

$$\sup_{t\in[0,T]} \|\mu(t) - \nu(t)\|_\infty < \|\mu_0 - \nu_0\|_\infty e^{QT} + 2\epsilon\left(\frac{e^{QT}-1}{Q}\right). \tag{114}$$

where $Q := (2n+1)H$ and $H := \max_{i\in I} \|U_i\|$.

Proof For each i in I and $t \geq 0$, let

$$\beta_i(a_i|\mu) := J_i(a_i, \mu_{-i}) - J_i(\mu_i, \mu_{-i}), \quad \beta_i^{\epsilon}(a_i|\nu_i) := J_i^{\epsilon}(a_i, \nu_{-i}) - J_i^{\epsilon}(\nu_i, \nu_{-i}),$$

and

$$F_i(\mu, E_i) := \int_{E_i} \beta_i(a_i|\mu)\mu_i(da_i), \quad F_i^{\epsilon}(\nu, E_i) := \int_{E_i} \beta_i^{\epsilon}(a_i|\nu)\nu_i(da_i).$$

Since U_i is bounded, by Lemma 42 there exists $Q > 0$ such that

$$\|F(\nu) - F(\mu)\|_\infty \leq Q\|\nu - \mu\|_\infty \quad \forall \mu, \nu \in \mathbb{P}(A_1) \times \cdots \times \mathbb{P}(A_n). \tag{115}$$

Actually, $Q := (2n + 1)H$ and $H := \max_{i \in I} \|U_i\|$. We also have that, for all $i \in I$ and $\nu \in \mathbb{P}(A_1) \times \cdots \times \mathbb{P}(A_n)$,

$$\|F_i(\nu) - F_i^{\epsilon}(\nu)\| \leq \int_{A_i} |\beta_i(a_i|\nu) - \beta_i^{\epsilon}(a_i|\nu)|\nu_i(da_i) \leq 2\|U_i - U_i^{\epsilon}\| \leq 2\epsilon,$$

so

$$\|F(\nu) - F^{\epsilon}(\nu)\|_\infty \leq 2\epsilon. \tag{116}$$

By Lemma 41 and (115)–(116) we have

$$\begin{aligned}
\frac{d\|\mu(t) - \nu(t)\|_\infty}{dt} &\leq \|\mu'(t) - \nu'(t)\|_\infty \\
&= \|F(\mu(t)) - F^{\epsilon}(\nu(t))\|_\infty \\
&\leq \|F(\mu(t)) - F(\nu(t))\|_\infty + \|F(\nu(t)) - F^{\epsilon}(\nu(t))\|_\infty \\
&\leq Q\|\mu(t) - \nu(t)\|_\infty + 2\epsilon.
\end{aligned}$$

Then

$$\frac{d\|\mu(t) - \nu(t)\|_\infty}{dt} - Q\|\mu(t) - \nu(t)\|_\infty \leq 2\epsilon.$$

Multiplying by e^{-Qt} we get

$$\frac{d\|\mu(t) - \nu(t)\|_\infty e^{-Qt}}{dt} - Q\|\mu(t) - \nu(t)\|_\infty e^{-Qt} \leq 2\epsilon e^{-Qt},$$

and integrating in the interval $[0, t]$, where $t \leq T$, we get

$$\|\mu(t) - \nu(t)\|_\infty e^{-Qt} - \|\mu_0 - \nu_0\|_\infty \leq 2\epsilon \left(\frac{1 - e^{-Qt}}{Q}\right).$$

Then for all $t \in [0, T]$

$$\begin{aligned}
\|\mu(t) - \nu(t)\|_\infty &= \|\mu_0 - \nu_0\|_\infty e^{Qt} + 2\epsilon \left(\frac{e^{Qt} - 1}{Q}\right) \\
&\leq \|\mu_0 - \nu_0\|_\infty e^{QT} + 2\epsilon \left(\frac{e^{QT} - 1}{Q}\right),
\end{aligned}$$

which yields (114). □

Remark 44 *The last argument in the proof of Theorem 43 is a particular case of the well-known Gronwall–Bellman inequality: If $f(\cdot)$ is nonnegative and $f'(t) \leq Qf(t) + c$ for all $t \geq 0$, where Q and c are nonnegative constants, then*

$$f(t) \leq f(0)e^{Qt} + cQ^{-1}(e^{Qt} - 1) \text{ for all } t \geq 0.$$

For the reader's convenience, we include the proof here.

From Theorem 43 we obtain the following corollary.

Corollary 45 *Let us assume the hypotheses of Theorem 43. Suppose that for each i in I, there exists a sequence of functions $\{U_i^{\epsilon_n}\}_{n=1}^{\infty}$ and vectors of probability measures $\{\nu^n\}_{n=1}^{\infty}$ such that $\max_{i \in I} \|U_i - U_i^{\epsilon_n}\| \to 0$ and $\|\mu_0 - \nu_0^n\|_\infty \to 0$. If $\mu(\cdot)$ and $\nu^n(\cdot)$ are solutions of (112) and (113), respectively, with initial conditions $\mu(0) = \mu_0$ and $\nu^n(0) = \nu_0^n$, then for $T < \infty$*

$$\lim_{n \to \infty} \sup_{t \in [0,T]} \|\mu(t) - \nu_n(t)\|_\infty = 0.$$

To end this section, we highlight the following two comments that are considered relevant for the application of Theorem 43.

Remark 46 (*i*) *As in Sections 5.1.1 and 5.1.2, consider a game with strategies in compact metric spaces. For each player $i \in I$ consider a partition P_{i,k_i} of A_i, and suppose that the initial condition $\mu_{i,0} \in \mathbb{P}(A_i)$ of (112) can be approximated in the variation norm by a discrete probability distribution $\mu_{k_i,0} \in \mathbb{P}(P_{i,k_i})$. Then for any $i \in I$ and $E_i \in \mathcal{B}(A_i) \cap P_{i,k_i}$, (113) can be written as in (109) (or (106)), with U_i^ϵ as in (108) (or (103)). So, in this particular case, (112) can be approximated by a system of differential equations in $\mathbb{R}^{2^{k_1}+\cdots+2^{k_n}}$ of the form (110).*

(*ii*) *For the existence of the replicator dynamics, only the boundedness of the payoff functions is necessary (see Proposition 11 in Section 3.3). So, the hypothesis of compactness on the set of strategies is not necessary in Theorem 43. Hence, the hypothesis of compactness on the set of strategies is also not necessary to approximate (112) by a finite dimensional dynamical system. For example, it is sufficient that there exists a discrete probability distribution with finite values for any probability distribution over the set of strategies. For this latter case, it is enough that for each $i \in I$, A_i be a separable metric space; see theorem 6.3, page 44 in Parthasarathy (1967). However, the compactness of the set of strategies ensures the existence of a Nash equilibrium.*

5.3 An Approximation Theorem in the Weak Form

The next approximation result, Theorem 50, establishes the proximity of two paths generated by two different dynamical systems (the original model and a discrete approximating model) with different initial conditions, under the weak topology. To this end we use the Kantorovich–Rubinstein norm $||\cdot||_{kr}$ (see (11)) on $\mathbb{M}(A)$, which metrizes the weak topology.

Remark 47 *Let A be a separable metric space. We say that a mapping $\mu\colon [0,\infty) \to \mathbb{M}(A)$ is* weakly differentiable *if there exists $\mu'(t) \in \mathbb{M}(A)$ such that, for every $t > 0$ and $g \in \mathbb{C}_B(A)$*

$$\lim_{\epsilon\to 0}\frac{1}{\epsilon}\left[\int_A g(a)\mu(t+\epsilon, da) - \int_A g(a)\mu(t, da)\right] = \int_A g(a)\mu'(t, da). \tag{117}$$

If $||\cdot||_{kr}$ is the Kantorovich–Rubinstein metric in (11), *then* (117) *is equivalent to*

$$\lim_{\epsilon\to 0}\left\|\frac{\mu(t+\epsilon)-\mu(t)}{\epsilon} - \mu'(t)\right\|_{kr} = 0. \tag{118}$$

Moreover if $\mu'(t)$ is the strong derivative *of $\mu(t)$, then it is also the* weak derivative *of $\mu(t)$. Conversely, if $\mu'(t)$ is the* weak derivative *of $\mu(t)$ and $\mu(t)$ is continuous in t with the total variation norm* (1), *then it is the* strong derivative *of $\mu(t)$. (See Heidergott and Leahu (2010).)*

Lemma 48 *For each i in I, let A_i be a separable metric space. If each map $\mu_i\colon [0,\infty) \to \mathbb{M}(A_i)$ is* strongly differentiable, *then*

$$\frac{d||\mu(t)||_\infty^{kr}}{dt} \le ||\mu'(t)||_\infty^{kr}.$$

Proof The proof is similar to that of Lemma 41. □

Lemma 49 *For each i in I, consider a bounded separable metric space (A_i, ϑ_i) (with diameter $C_i > 0$), and the metric space $(A_1\times\cdots\times A_n, \vartheta^*)$, where $\vartheta^*(a,b) = \max_{i\in I}\{\vartheta_i(a_i,b_i)\}$ for any a, b in $A_1\times\cdots\times A_n$. Let $F(\cdot)$ be as in* (46)–(47) *(with $F_i(\cdot)$ as in* (50)*). For each i in I, suppose that the payoff function $U_i(\cdot)$ in* (18) *is bounded and satisfies that $||U_i||_L < \infty$, where $||\cdot||_L$ is defined in* (8). *Then there exists $Q > 0$ such that*

$$||F(\nu) - F(\mu)||_\infty^{kr} \le Q||\nu - \mu||_\infty^{kr} \tag{119}$$

for all $\mu, \nu \in \mathbb{P}(A_1)\times\cdots\times\mathbb{P}(A_n) \cap \mathbb{M}_K(A_1)\times\cdots\times\mathbb{M}_K(A_n)$, where $Q := [2H + (2n-1)CH_L]$, $H := \max_{i\in I}||U_i||$, $H_L := \max_{i\in I}||U_i||_L$, and $C := \max_{i\in I} C_i$.

Proof See Section 3.3 of the online appendix. □

Theorem 50 *For each i in I, let* (A_i, ϑ_i) *be a bounded separable metric space (with diameter* $C_i > 0$*), and* $U_i, U_i^\epsilon : A_1 \times \cdots \times A_n \to \mathbb{R}$ *be two bounded functions such that* $\max_{i \in I} \|U_i - U_i^\epsilon\| < \epsilon$*. For each i in I, suppose that* $\|U_i\|_L < \infty$ *(where* $\|\cdot\|_L$ *is defined in* (8)*) and consider the replicator dynamics induced by* $\{U_i\}_{i=1}^n$ *and* $\{U_i^\epsilon\}_{i=1}^n$*, as in* (112) *and* (113)*. If* $\mu(\cdot)$ *and* $\nu(\cdot)$ *are solutions of* (112) *and* (113)*, respectively, with initial conditions* $\mu(0) = \mu_0$ *and* $\nu(0) = \nu_0$*, then for* $T < \infty$

$$\sup_{t \in [0,T]} \|\mu(t) - \nu(t)\|_\infty^{kr} < \|\mu_0 - \nu_0\|_\infty^{kr} e^{QT} + 2\epsilon \left(\frac{e^{QT} - 1}{Q} \right). \tag{120}$$

where $Q := [2H + (2n-1)CH_L]$*,* $H := \max_{i \in I} \|U_i\|$*,* $H_L := \max_{i \in I} \|U_i\|_L$*, and* $C := \max_{i \in I} C_i$.

Proof For each i in I and $t \geq 0$, let

$$\beta_i(a_i|\mu) := J_i(a_i, \mu_i) - J_i(\mu_i, \mu_{-i}), \quad \beta_i^\epsilon(a_i|\nu_i) := J_i^\epsilon(a_i, \nu_{-i}) - J_i^\epsilon(\nu_i, \nu_{-i}),$$

and

$$F_i(\mu, E_i) := \int_{E_i} \beta_i(a_i|\mu)\mu_i(da_i), \quad F_i^\epsilon(\nu, E_i) := \int_{E_i} \beta_i^\epsilon(a_i|\nu)\nu_i(da_i).$$

By Lemma 49 there exists $Q > 0$ such that

$$\|F(\nu) - F(\mu)\|_\infty^{kr} \leq Q\|\nu - \mu\|_\infty^{kr} \tag{121}$$

for all $\mu, \nu \in \mathbb{P}(A_1) \times \cdots \times \mathbb{P}(A_n) \cap \mathbb{M}_K(A_1) \times \cdots \times \mathbb{M}_K(A_n)$. Actually, $Q := [2H + (2n-1)CH_L]$, $H := \max_{i \in I} \|U_i\|$, $H_L := \max_{i \in I} \|U_i\|_L$, and $C := \max_{i \in I} C_i$.

We also have that, for all i in I and

$$\nu \in \mathbb{P}(A_1) \times \cdots \times \mathbb{P}(A_n) \cap \mathbb{M}_K(A_1) \times \cdots \times \mathbb{M}_K(A_n),$$

$$\begin{aligned}
\|F_i(\nu) - F_i^\epsilon(\nu)\|_{kr} &\leq \sup_{\substack{\|f\|_L \leq 1 \\ f(a_i^0)=0}} \int_{A_i} f(a_i)|\beta_i(a_i|\nu) - \beta_i^\epsilon(a_i|\nu)|\nu_i(da_i) \\
&\leq 2\|U_i - U_i^\epsilon\| \sup_{\substack{\|f\|_L \leq 1 \\ f(a_i^0)=0}} \int_{A_i} f(a_i)\nu_i(da_i) \\
&\leq 2C\epsilon.
\end{aligned}$$

Then[2]

$$\|F(\nu) - F^{\epsilon}(\nu)\|_{\infty}^{kr} \le 2C\epsilon \tag{122}$$

By Lemma 48 and (121)–(122) we have

$$\begin{aligned}\frac{d\|\mu(t) - \nu(t)\|_{\infty}^{kr}}{dt} &\le \|\mu'(t) - \nu'(t)\|_{\infty}^{kr} \\ &= \|F(\mu(t)) - F^{\epsilon}(\nu(t))\|_{\infty}^{kr} \\ &\le \|F(\mu(t)) - F(\nu(t))\|_{\infty}^{kr} + \|F(\nu(t)) - F^{\epsilon}(\nu(t))\|_{\infty}^{kr} \\ &\le Q\|\mu(t) - \nu(t)\|_{\infty}^{kr} + 2C\epsilon.\end{aligned}$$

(See the Remark 44 after Theorem 43.) The rest of the proof is similar to that done in Theorem 43. □

Corollary 51 *Let us assume the hypotheses of Theorem 50. Suppose that for each i in I, there exist sequences of functions* $\{U_i^{\epsilon_n}\}_{n=1}^{\infty}$ *and of vectors of probability measures* $\{\nu^n\}_{n=1}^{\infty}$ *such that* $\max_{i\in I} \|U_i - U_i^{\epsilon_n}\| \to 0$ *and* $\|\mu_0 - \nu_0^n\|_{\infty}^{kr} \to 0$. *If* $\mu(\cdot)$ *and* $\nu^n(\cdot)$ *are solutions of* (112) *and* (113), *respectively, with initial conditions* $\mu(0) = \mu_0$ *and* $\nu^n(0) = \nu_0^n$, *then, for* $T < \infty$,

$$\lim_{n\to\infty} \sup_{t\in[0,T]} \|\mu(t) - \nu_n(t)\|_{\infty}^{kr} = 0.$$

To end this section, we highlight the following note that is considered relevant for the application of Theorem 50.

Remark 52 *As in Sections 5.1.1 and 5.1.2, consider a game with strategies in compact metric spaces. For each player* $i \in I$, *let* $\|U_i\|_L < \infty$ *and consider a partition* P_{k_i} *of* A_i. *Suppose that the initial condition* $\mu_{i,0} \in \mathbb{P}(A_i)$ *of* (112) *can be approximated in the weak form by a discrete probability distribution* $\mu_{k_i,0} \in \mathbb{P}(P_{k_i})$. *Then for any* $i \in I$ *and* $E_i \in \mathcal{B}(A_i) \cap P_{k_i}$, (113) *can be written as in* (109) *(or* (106)*), with* U_i^{ϵ} *as in* (108) *(or* (103)*). So, in this particular case,* (112) *can be approximated by a system of differential equations in* $\mathbb{R}^{2^{k_1}+\cdots+2^{k_n}}$ *of the form* (110).

---

[2] Note that if f satisfies that $\|f\|_L \le 1$ and $f(a_i^0) = 0$, then $f(a_i) \le \vartheta_i(a_i, a_i^0) \le C_i$ for all $a_i \in A_i$. Therefore $\sup_{\substack{\|f\|_L\le 1\\ f(a_i^0)=0}} \int_{A_i} f(a_i)\nu_i(da_i) \le C.$

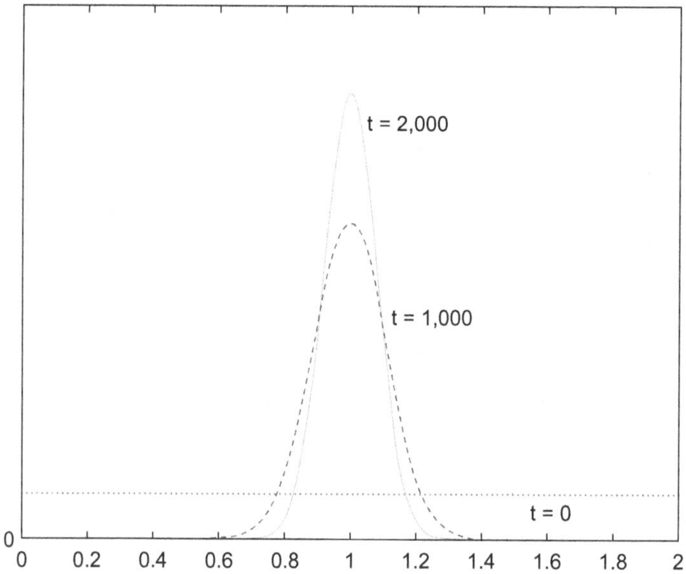

Figure 1 Linear-quadratic model: symmetric case.

5.4 Examples

5.4.1 A Linear-Quadratic Model: Symmetric Case

Consider the symmetric form of the game in Section 2.2, as was done in Section 4.5.1. Let $A = [0, M]$, for $M > 0$, be the strategy set and we rewrite the payoff functions (26) and (27) as

$$U(x, y) = -ax^2 - bxy + cx + dy,$$

with $a, b, c > 0$ and d any real number. If $2c(a - b) > 0$ and $4a^2 - b^2 > 0$, then we have an interior NES

$$x^* = \frac{2c(a-b)}{4a^2 - b^2}.$$

In Section 4.5.1 it is proved that this NES $x^* \equiv \delta_{x^*}$ is r-SUS. Moreover, we have that $\mu(t) \to \delta_{x^*}$ in distribution.

Consider a game where $a = 2$, $b = 1$, $c = 5$, $d = 1$, $M = 2$. For this game the payoff function $U(\cdot, \cdot)$ is bounded Lipschitz and by Theorem 50 we can approximate the replicator dynamics by a finite-dimensional dynamical system of the form (107) under the Kantorovich–Rubinstein norm. Figure 1 shows a numerical approximation for this game where the Nash equilibrium is $x^* = 1$. For this numerical approximation we consider a partition with 100 elements with the same size, and use the forward Euler method for solving ordinary differential equations. We consider the uniform distribution as initial condition. We show the distribution at times 0, 1000, and 2000.

Note that, under the strong norm (1), the Nash equilibrium $x^* = 1$ cannot be approximated by any probability measure with continuous density function.

5.4.2 Graduated Risk Game

As in Section 4.5.2, consider the game in Section 2.6. Section 4.5.2 shows that if $v < c$ in the payoff function (37), that is,

$$U(x,y) = \begin{cases} vy + \frac{v-c}{2}(1-y) & \text{if } y > x, \\ \frac{v-c}{2}(1-x) & \text{if } y \le x, \end{cases}$$

then the NES μ^* in (38) with density function

$$\frac{d\mu^*(x)}{dx} = \frac{\alpha-1}{2} x^{\frac{\alpha-3}{2}}$$

is a r-SUS for any metric r in $\mathbb{P}(A)$, with $A = [0,1]$.

Let $\mu(t)$ be the solution of the symmetric replicator dynamics induced by $U(\cdot,\cdot)$ in (37). Then, as in Section 4.5.2, for any initial condition μ_0 with support [0,1], we have that if $K(\mu_0, \mu^*) < \varphi'(\epsilon) = \left(\frac{\epsilon}{2}\right)^2$, then

(*i*) $\mu(t) \in \mathcal{W}_{\varphi'(\epsilon)}(\mu^*)$ for all $t \ge 0$;
(*ii*) $\|\mu(t) - \mu^*\| < \epsilon$ for all $t \ge 0$;
(*iii*) $r_w(\mu(t), \mu^*) < \epsilon$ for all $t \ge 0$.

Consider a game where $c = 10$, $v = 6.5$. For this game, the payoff function $U(\cdot,\cdot)$ in (37) is bounded, and by Theorem 43 we can approximate the replicator dynamics by a finite-dimensional dynamical system of the form (107) under the strong norm (1). Figure 2 shows a numerical approximation for this game. For this approximation we consider a partition with 100 elements with the same size and use the forward Euler method for solving ordinary differential equations. We consider the uniform distribution as initial condition. We show the distribution at times 0, 500, and 1000.

In the same way, Figure 3 shows a numerical approximation for a game where $c = 10$, $v = 0.5$. For this approximation we consider a partition with 100 elements with the same size, and use the forward Euler method for solving ordinary differential equations. We consider the uniform distribution as initial condition. We show the distribution at times 0, 500, and 1000.

5.4.3 War of Attrition Game

Consider the game in Section 2.7. Section 4.5.3 shows that if $v \le m$ in the payoff function (40), that is,

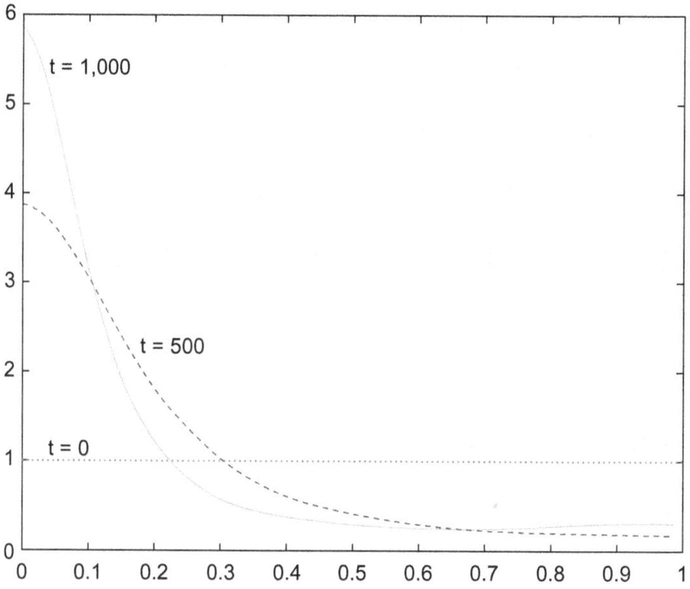

Figure 2 Graduated risk game with $c = 10,\ v = 6.5$.

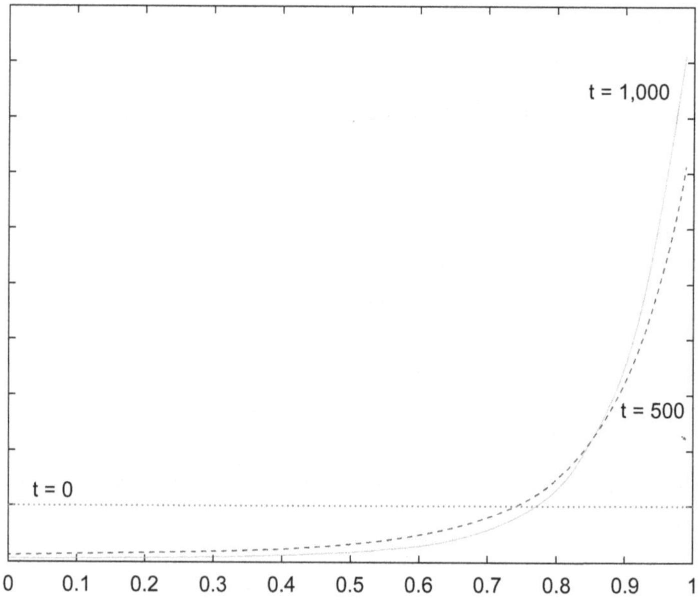

Figure 3 Graduated risk game with $c = 10,\ v = 0.5$.

$$U(x,y) = \begin{cases} v - y & \text{if } y < x, \\ \frac{v}{2} - y & \text{if } y = x, \\ -x & \text{if } y > x, \end{cases}$$

then the NES μ^* with density function (41), namely,

$$\frac{d\mu^*(x)}{dx} = \begin{cases} \frac{1}{v}e^{-x/v} & \text{if } x \in \left[0, m - \frac{v}{2}\right], \\ 0 & \text{if } x \in \left(m - \frac{v}{2}, m\right), \\ \text{a weight } \delta_m \cdot e^{1/2 - m/v} & \text{at the atom } \{m\}, \end{cases}$$

is a r-SUS for any metric r in $\mathbb{P}(A)$, with $A = [0, m]$.

Let $\mu(t)$ be the solution of the symmetric replicator dynamics induced by $U(\cdot,\cdot)$ in (40). Section 4.5.3 shows that for any initial condition μ_0 with support [0,1] we have that, if $K(\mu_0, \mu^*) < \varphi'(\epsilon) = \left(\frac{\epsilon}{2}\right)^2$, then

(*i*) $\mu(t) \in \mathcal{W}_{\varphi'(\epsilon)}(\mu^*)$ for all $t \geq 0$;
(*ii*) $\|\mu(t) - \mu^*\| < \frac{\epsilon}{m}$ for all $t \geq 0$;
(*iii*) $r_w(\mu(t), \mu^*) < \epsilon$ for all $t \geq 0$.

Consider a game where $m = 10$, $v = 4$. For this game the payoff function $U(\cdot,\cdot)$ in (40) is bounded and the NES μ^* is given by the density function

$$\frac{d\mu^*(x)}{dx} = \begin{cases} \frac{e^{-x/4}}{4} & \text{if } x \in [0, 8], \\ 0 & \text{if } x \in (8, 10), \\ \text{a weight } \delta_{10} \cdot e^{-2} & \text{at the atom } \{10\}. \end{cases}$$

Using Theorem 43, we can approximate the replicator dynamics by a finite-dimensional dynamical system of the form (107) under the strong norm (1). Figure 4 shows a numerical approximation for this game. For this numerical approximation we consider a partition with 100 elements with the same size, and use the forward Euler method for solving ordinary differential equations. We consider the uniform distribution as initial condition. We show the distribution at times 0, 100, and 600.

5.5 Comments

In this section, we established conditions to approximate the replicator dynamics in a measure space by a sequence of dynamical systems on finite-dimensional spaces. We also presented three examples. The first one may be applicable to oligopoly models, theory of international trade, and public good models. The second and third examples deal with a graduated risk game and a war of attrition game, respectively.

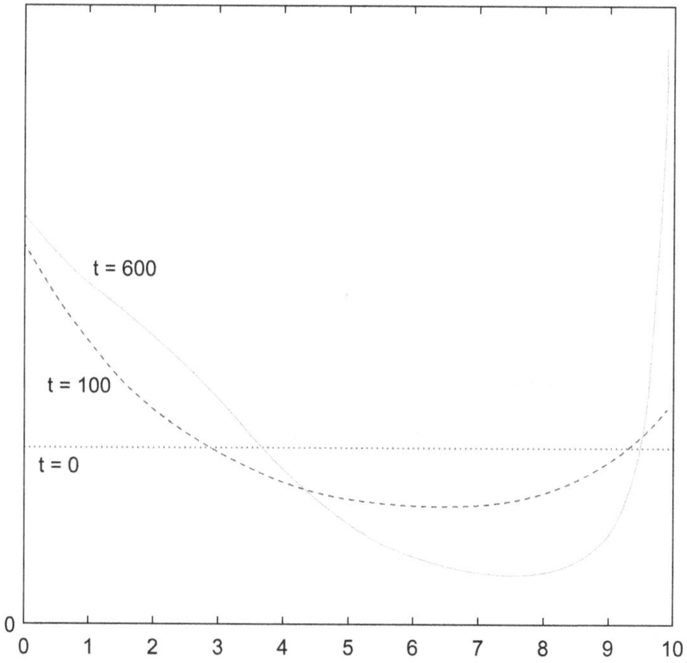

Figure 4 War of attrition game $m = 10,\ v = 4$.

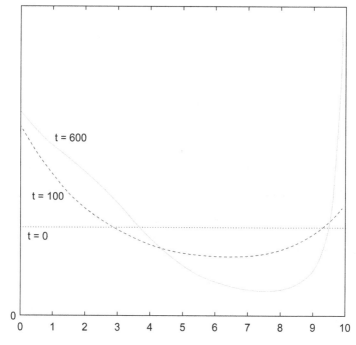

There are many questions, however, that remain open. For instance, the replicator dynamics has been studied in other general spaces without direct applications in game theory such as Kravvaritis et al. (2008, 2010, 2011) and Kravvaritis and Papanicolaou (2011). Papanicolaou and Smyrlis (2009) studied conditions for stability and examples for these general cases. These extensions may be applicable in areas such as migration, regional sciences, and spatial economics (see Fujita et al. (2001), chapters 5 and 6). An open question: Can we establish conditions to approximate the replicator dynamics for general spaces by a sequence of dynamical systems on finite-dimensional spaces?

In the theory of evolutionary games there are several interesting dynamics, for instance, the imitation dynamics, the monotone-selection dynamics, the best-response dynamics, the Brown–von Neumann–Nash dynamics, and so forth (see, for instance, Hofbauer and Sigmund (1998, 2003), Sandholm (2010)). Some of these evolutionary dynamics have been extended to games with strategies in spaces of probability measures. For instance, Hofbauer et al. (2009) extend the Brown–von Neumann–Nash dynamics; Lahkar and Riedel (2015) extend the logit dynamics. These publications establish conditions for the existence of solutions and the stability of the corresponding dynamical systems. Cheung (2014) proposes a general theory for pairwise comparison dynamics, and for imitative dynamics in Cheung (2016). Ruijgrok and Ruijgrok (2015) extend the replicator dynamics with a mutation term. An open question: Can we establish conditions to approximate other evolutionary dynamics for measurable spaces by a sequence of finite-dimensional dynamical systems?

6 The Replicator Dynamics as a Deterministic Approximation

In this section we study the replicator dynamics as the limit of a sequence of Markov processes. There are many references (mentioned in Section 1.1) on this issue when the strategy space is finite. However, a more general mathematical structure is needed if the strategy set is a measurable space, which we consider in this section. We use a general theorem (Kolokoltsov (2006)) in which an infinite-dimensional kinetic equation (a differential equation on a space of measures) is a limit of a sequence of jump Markov process.

Section 6.1 presents notation and technical requirements. Section 6.2 shows a technique proposed by Kolokoltsov (2006, 2010) to approximate a sequence of pure-jump models of binary interaction (in a Banach space) by means of a deterministic dynamical system. Section 6.3 uses techniques of Section 6.2 to establish conditions under which the replicator dynamics are a limit of a sequence of Markov processes. Finally, Section 6.4 presents some general comments on future perspectives.

6.1 Technical Preliminaries

In this section we summarize some facts about the approximation of ordinary differential equations by Markov processes and other related topics. For proofs we refer to Kallenberg (2002), Ethier and Kurtz (1984), and Böttcher et al. (2013).

6.1.1 Markov Processes

Let F be a Banach space, and $L(F)$ the set of all linear bounded operators from F into itself. A *strongly continuous semigroup* of linear operators on F is a mapping $T\colon [0,\infty) \to L(F)$ such that

(*i*) $T(t+s) = T(t)T(s)$ for all $t, s \geq 0$, with $T(0) = I$, where I is the identity operator.
(*ii*) $\lim_{t\to 0+} T(t)x = x$ in the strong operator topology.

Definition 53 *The generator G of a strongly continuous semigroup $T(\cdot)$ is defined as follows. Let*

$$\mathcal{D}(G) := \left\{ f \in F: \lim_{t \to 0+} \left[\frac{T(t) - I}{t} \right] f \text{ exists} \right\},$$

and for $f \in \mathcal{D}(G)$ *let*

$$Gf := \lim_{t \to 0+} \left[\frac{T(t) - I}{t} \right] f.$$

The connection of linear semigroup theory with Markov processes is as follows. Let A be a locally compact metric space. Let $x(\cdot) = \{x(t): t \geq 0\}$ be a Markov process with values in A and transition probability function $P(s, x, t, E)$, namely,

$$P(s, x, t, E) = P(x(t) \in E \mid x(s) = x)$$

for all $t \geq s \geq 0$, $x \in A$, and $E \in \mathcal{B}(A)$. Let F be the linear space of real-valued measurable functions f on $[0, \infty) \times A$ such that

$$\int_A |f(t, y)| P(s, x, t, dy) \leq \infty$$

for each $t \geq s \geq 0$ and $x \in A$. For each $t \geq 0$ and $f \in F$, let $T_t f$ be a function on $[0, \infty) \times A$ defined by

$$T_t f(s, x) := \int_A f(s + t, y) P(s, x, s + t, dy).$$

In this case the operators T_t, $t \geq 0$, form a semigroup of operators on F.

Let $\mathbb{C}_\infty(A)$ be the space of continuous functions vanishing at infinity.[3] A Markov process is called *time-homogeneous* if $P(s, x, s + t, E) = P(0, x, t, E)$ for all $s \geq 0$. A (time-homogeneous) Markov process in a locally compact metric space A is said to be a Feller process if for any $f \in \mathbb{C}_\infty(A)$ we have that $T_t f \in \mathbb{C}_\infty(A)$.

6.1.2 Approximation of Pure-Jump Process

A Markov jump process describes a continuous-time stochastic process such that, intuitively, it behaves as follows. Consider that the system starts from a point $x(s) = x \in A$ for some time $s \geq 0$. The process stays in the state x for a random length of time τ_1 and then instantaneously "jumps" to a new state $y \neq x$. It stays there a random length of time τ_2 (independent of τ_1) and then "jumps" to a new state $z \neq y$, and this behavior is repeated indefinitely.

[3] $\mathbb{C}_\infty(A)$ is the set of real-valued continuous functions such that for every $\epsilon > 0$ there exists a compact set $K \subset A$ that satisfies $\sup_{a \notin K} |f(a)| \leq \epsilon$.

By a pure-jump (*time-homogeneous*) Markov process on A we mean a Markov process with a generator of the form

$$Gf(x) = \int_A [f(y) - f(x)]Q(x, dy),$$

for f in $\mathbb{C}_\infty(A)$, where Q is a transition kernel, that is, for every $x \in A$ and $E \in \mathcal{B}(A)$, $Q(\cdot, E)$ is a real-valued measurable function, and $Q(x, \cdot)$ is a signed measure on $\mathcal{B}(A)$. In particular, for pure-jump processes Q satisfies that $Q(x,x) = 0$ and $Q(x,A) < \infty$ for every $x \in A$.

Let A be a complete separable metric space with metric ϑ. Consider $\{x_n(\cdot)\}$ a sequence of pure-jump Markov processes in A. We say that this sequence *converges weakly* to a Markov process $x(\cdot)$ if the distribution law of $\{x_n(\cdot)\}$ converges weakly to the distribution law of $\{x(\cdot)\}$.

The following theorem gives the solution of some ordinary differential equations as the limit of a sequence of pure-jump Markov processes.

Proposition 54 *Let $A \subset \mathbb{R}^m$ (endowed with the Euclidean norm $|\cdot|$), and let $\{x_n(t)\}$ be a sequence of pure-jump Markov processes in A such that for every $n = 1, 2, \ldots$, the process $x_n(\cdot)$ has the generator*

$$G_n f(x) = \int_A [f(y) - f(x)]Q_n(x, dy)$$

and $x_n(0) = x_0$. For every $n = 1, 2, \ldots$ and x in A, consider the functions

$$F_n(x) := \int_A |x - y|Q_n(x, dy) \quad \text{and} \quad H_n(x) := \int_{|x-y|>\epsilon_n} |x - y|Q_n(x, dy),$$

where $\{\epsilon_n\}$ is a sequence of positive numbers such that $\lim_{n\to\infty} \epsilon_n = 0$. Consider the differential equation

$$x'(t) = G(x(t)), \quad \text{with } x(0) = x_0, \tag{123}$$

where G satisfies a Lipschitz condition. Finally, assume that, for every $x \in A$,

(*i*) $\sup_n \sup_{x\in A} F_n(x) < \infty$,
(*ii*) $\lim_{n\to\infty} \sup_{x\in A} H_n(x) = 0$.

If $G_n I(\cdot) := \int_A [y - (\cdot)]Q_n(\cdot, dy)$ converges uniformly to $G(\cdot)$, then the sequence of stochastic processes $x_n(\cdot)$ converges weakly to the solution $x(\cdot)$ of the differential equation (123)*. Moreover, for every $\epsilon > 0$ and $t > 0$,*

$$\lim_{n\to\infty} P(\sup_{s\le t} |x_n(s) - x(s)| > \epsilon) = 0.$$

Proof See Kurtz (1970, 1971). □

Proposition 54 is, in fact, a particular case of a theorem on convergence of Feller processes (see Kallenberg (2002), chapter 19).

Let A be a compact metric space. Then $\mathbb{M}(A)$ (endowed with the weak topology) is a locally compact metric space (see Li (2010)). Under this condition, we can talk about a Markov process with state spaces in $\mathbb{M}(A)$. This Markov process is called a measure-valued Markov process. For references on this general case see, for example, Li (2010), Dynkin (1994), and Kolokoltsov (2010).

In Section 6.2 we see the replicator dynamics as the limit of a sequence of measure-valued Markov processes.

6.1.3 Notation

Let A be a separable and compact metric space, and consider the Cartesian products $A^j := A \times \cdots \times A$ (j-times) and $A^\infty := A \times A \times \cdots$ (infinite-times) with their product topologies. We shall denote by $A^\sqcup$ the disjoint union of the sets A^j, namely, $A^\sqcup = \sqcup_{j=1}^\infty A^j$, [4] and which is a separable and locally compact space.

For the following definition we consider the set $\mathbb{N}$ of natural numbers.

Definition 55 *A measure μ in $\mathbb{M}(A^\infty)$ is called* symmetric *if for any permutation $\rho: \mathbb{N} \to \mathbb{N}$ that replaces only finitely many elements, we have*

$$\mu(\rho E) = \mu(E) \quad \forall E \in \mathcal{B}(A^\infty),$$

where

$$\rho E := \Big\{(a_1, a_2, \ldots, a_j, \ldots) \in A^\infty : (a_{\rho(1)}, a_{\rho(2)}, \ldots, a_{\rho(j),\ldots}) \in E\Big\}.$$

The set of symmetric measures *on A^∞ is written as $\mathbb{M}_S(A^\infty)$.*

Similarly, as in Definition 55, we can define a *symmetric measure* on A^j and $A^\sqcup$. The spaces of symmetric measures on A^j and $A^\sqcup$ will be denoted by $\mathbb{M}_S(A^j)$ and $\mathbb{M}_S(A^\sqcup)$, respectively. For more details about symmetric measures see Hewitt and Savage (1955) and Bogachev (2007) (chapter 10).

Let X be either A^j , A^∞, or $A^\sqcup$. The spaces of positive measures, and symmetric positive measures on X will be denoted by $\mathbb{M}^+(X)$ and $\mathbb{M}_S^+(X)$, respectively.

A function f: $A^\infty \to \mathbb{R}$ is said to be *symmetric* if for any permutation $\rho: \mathbb{N} \to \mathbb{N}$ and $(a_1, a_2, \ldots, a_j, \ldots)$ in A^∞

$$f(a_1, a_2, \ldots, a_j, \ldots) = f(a_{\rho(1)}, a_{\rho(2)}, \ldots, a_{\rho(j)}, \ldots).$$

[4] $\sqcup_{j=1}^\infty A^j = \cup_{j=1}^\infty \{(a, j) : a \in A^j\}$

A real-valued *symmetric function* on A^j and $A^{\sqcup}$ is defined similarly. Let X be either A^j, A^{∞}, or $A^{\sqcup}$. We shall denote by $\mathbb{B}_S(X)$ (resp. $\mathbb{C}_S(X)$) the Banach space of symmetric bounded (resp. continuous) real-valued functions on X.

On X we consider the equivalence relation $\sim$ given by

$$(a_1, a_2, \ldots, a_j, \ldots) \sim (b_1, b_2, \ldots, b_j, \ldots)$$

if and only if there exists a permutation ρ such that $b_i = a_{\rho(i)}$ for all $i = 1, 2, \ldots$. Let X_S be the quotient space (the space of equivalence classes) with the quotient topology (for details, see Pedersen (2012), chapter 1). This allows us to identify, for example, $\mathbb{C}_S(X) = \mathbb{C}(X_S)$.

6.2 Pure-Jump Markov Processes for Binary Interacting Individuals

In this section we see how a sequence of general pure-jump Markov processes converges weakly to the solution of an infinite-dimensional differential equation (called a kinetic equation). For details see Kolokoltsov (2006) and Kolokoltsov (2010). In particular, we are interested in pure-jump Markov processes that emerge from the interaction of two particles, in other words, that originate from binary interacting particles.

In game theory, we are interested in the behavior of individuals, which is why we replace the word "particles" (used in physical theory) with "individuals."

Let A be a separable and compact metric space. The symmetrical laws on A^j (which are uniquely defined by their projections to A^j_S) are called exchangeable systems of j individuals. The elements of $\mathbb{M}^+_S(A^{\sqcup})$ and $\mathbb{C}_S(A^{\sqcup})$ are called, respectively, the states and observables for a Markov process Z_t on $A^{\sqcup}$. We shall denote the elements of $A^{\sqcup}$ by bold letters, for example, **a**,**b**. A key observation from the theory of measure-valued limits is the inclusion of $A^{\sqcup}_S$ to $\mathbb{M}^+(A)$ given by

$$\mathbf{a} = (a_1, \ldots, a_l) \mapsto h\delta_{a_1} + \cdots + h\delta_{a_l}, \qquad h > 0, \tag{124}$$

which defines a bijection between $A^{\sqcup}_S$ and the space $\mathbb{M}^+_{h\delta}(A) \subset \mathbb{M}^+(A)$ of finite linear combinations of δ-measures.

For each $f \in \mathbb{B}_S(A^{\sqcup})$ and $\mathbf{a} = (a_1, \ldots, a_j) \in A^j \subset A^{\sqcup}$, we write $f(\mathbf{a}) = f(a_1, \ldots, a_j)$, $f^+(\mathbf{a}) = f^+(a_1, \ldots, a_j) = f(a_1) + \cdots + f(a_j)$, and $f^{\times}(\mathbf{a}) = f^{\times}(a_1, \ldots, a_j) = f(a_1) \cdot \cdots \cdot f(a_j)$. For a subset $I = \{i_1, i_2\}$ of two elements of a finite set $J = \{1, 2, \ldots, j\}$ we denote by I^c its complement $I^c = J - I$. Then for $\mathbf{a} = (a_1, \ldots, a_j) \in A^{\sqcup}$, $\mathbf{a}_I = (a_{i_1}, a_{i_2})$ and $\mathbf{a}_{I^c} = (a_{i^c_1}, \ldots, a_{i^c_m})$, where $I^c = \{i^c_1, \ldots, i^c_m\}$, and $\mathbf{a} = (\mathbf{a}_I, \mathbf{a}_{I^c})$.

By a pure jump process Z_t on $A^{\sqcup}$ that describes the interaction of two individuals, we mean a Markov process with a generator of the form

$$Gf(\mathbf{a}) = \sum_{I \subset \{1,2,..j\}} \int_{A^{\sqcup}} \left[f(\mathbf{a}_{I^c}, \mathbf{b}) - f(\mathbf{a}) \right] Q(\mathbf{a}_I, d\mathbf{b}), \tag{125}$$

where the binary-interaction transition kernel is such that

$$Q(\mathbf{a}_I) = \int_{A^{\sqcup}} Q(\mathbf{a}_I, d\mathbf{b}) = \sum_{m=1}^{\infty} \int_{A^m} Q_m(\mathbf{a}_I, db_1 \cdots db_m). \tag{126}$$

Changing the state space according to the mapping (124) yields the corresponding Markov process Z_t^h on $\mathbb{M}_{h\delta}^{+}(A)$. To this end, we scale the empirical measures $\delta_{\mathbf{a}} := \delta_{a_1} + \cdots + \delta_{a_l}$ by a factor $h > 0$ and use the bijection (124) to evaluate the map $\delta_{\mathbf{a}} \to f$. To each empirical measure $\delta_{\mathbf{a}}$ we assign a transition probability Q (this allows us to have a mean-field interaction). Finally, we scale the generator by the factor $h > 0$. The preceding change of space leads (125) to the generator G_h defined by (for details see Kolokoltsov (2006))

$$G_h f(h\delta_{\mathbf{a}}) = h \sum_{I \subset \{1,2,\ldots,j\}} \int_{A^{\sqcup}} \left[f(h\delta_{\mathbf{a}} - h\delta_{\mathbf{a}_I} + h\delta_{\mathbf{b}}) - f(h\delta_{\mathbf{a}}) \right] Q(h\delta_{\mathbf{a}}, \mathbf{a}_I, d\mathbf{b}). \tag{127}$$

Using the relation

$$\sum_{I \subset \{1,2,\ldots,j\}} f(\mathbf{a}_I) = \frac{1}{2} \sum_{i \in \{1,2,\ldots,j\}} \sum_{k \in \{1,2,\ldots,j\}} f(a_i, a_k) - \frac{1}{2} \sum_{i \in \{1,2,\ldots,j\}} f(a_i, a_i)$$
$$= \frac{1}{2} \int_{A^2} f(a_1, a_2) \delta_{\mathbf{a}}(da_1) \delta_{\mathbf{a}}(da_2) - \frac{1}{2} \int_A f(a, a) \delta_{\mathbf{a}}(da),$$

which holds for any symmetric f and $\mathbf{a} = (a_1, \ldots, a_j)$, we can express (127) as

$$G_h f(h\delta_{\mathbf{a}}) = \frac{1}{2}\frac{1}{h} \int_{A^{\sqcup}} \int_{A^2} \left[f(h\delta_{\mathbf{a}} - h\delta_{\mathbf{a}_I} + h\delta_{\mathbf{b}}) - f(h\delta_{\mathbf{a}}) \right] Q(h\delta_{\mathbf{a}}, (a_1, a_2), d\mathbf{b}) h\delta_{\mathbf{a}}(da_1) h\delta_{\mathbf{a}}(da_2)$$
$$- \frac{1}{2} \int_{A^{\sqcup}} \int_A \left[f(h\delta_{\mathbf{a}} - h\delta_{\mathbf{a}_I} + h\delta_{\mathbf{b}}) - f(h\delta_{\mathbf{a}}) \right] Q(h\delta_{\mathbf{a}}, (a, a), d\mathbf{b}) h\delta_{\mathbf{a}}(da).$$

Then, applying the operator (127) over the linear function

$$f_g(\mu) = \langle g, \mu \rangle = \int_A g(a) \mu(da) \qquad g \in \mathbb{C}(A), \tag{128}$$

we obtain

$$G_h f_g(h\delta_{\mathbf{a}})$$
$$= \frac{1}{2}\int_{A^{\sqcup}}\int_{A^2}\left[g^{+}(\mathbf{b}) - g^{+}(a_1,a_2)\right]Q(h\delta_{\mathbf{a}},(a_1,a_2),d\,\mathbf{b})h\delta_{\mathbf{a}}(da_1)h\delta_{\mathbf{a}}(da_2)$$
$$-\frac{1}{2}h\int_{A^{\sqcup}}\int_{A}\left[g^{+}(\mathbf{b}) - g^{+}(a,a)\right]Q(h\delta_{\mathbf{a}},(a,a),d\,\mathbf{b})h\delta_{\mathbf{a}}(da), \tag{129}$$

where $g^{+}(\mathbf{b}) = g^{+}(b_1,b_2,\ldots,b_k) = g(b_1) + g(b_2) + \ldots + g(b_k)$, and similarly for $g^{+}(a_1,a_2)$. For more details see Kolokoltsov (2006) and (2010) (chapter I).

Assume that the value of h is the scale or genetic relevance of each individual. This genetic relevance is decreasing, for example, with respect to the number of individuals, namely, if the population tends to infinity, then $h \to 0$. The genetic relevance of each individual h is high, for example, in small populations or endangered populations. When the scale or genetic relevance of each individual h is small (e.g. in a huge population) then the mass distribution $h\delta_{\mathbf{a}}$ retains this genetic relevance h. It follows that if h tends to 0 and $h\delta_{\mathbf{a}}$ tends to some distribution or probability measure μ, the corresponding generator G_h evaluated in (128)–(129)) tends to

$$Gf_g(\mu) = \frac{1}{2}\int_{A^{\sqcup}}\int_{A^2}\left[g^{+}(\mathbf{b}) - g^{+}(a_1,a_2)\right]Q(\mu,(a_1,a_2),d\,\mathbf{b})\mu(da_1)\mu(da_2). \tag{130}$$

Under some hypotheses (see Kolokoltsov (2006)), if $\mu(t)$ is a solution of the differential equation

$$\frac{d}{dt}\langle g,\mu(t)\rangle = Gf_g(\mu(t)) \quad \forall g \in \mathbb{C}(A_S), \quad (\text{with } \mu(0) = \mu_0), \tag{131}$$

then there exists a subsequence of stochastic processes $Z^{h_n}(t)$ (subfamily of $\{Z^h(t)\}_{h>0}$) with generator (127)–(129)), which converges weakly to $\mu(t)$.

6.3 The Replicator Dynamics as a Deterministic Approximation

In this section we specify a Markov game that can be approximated by the replicator dynamics. This Markov game models a stochastic interaction between individuals which explains the evolution of the probability distribution of characteristics in a population.

Suppose that in each stage of the game we select a pair of individuals of characteristics $a_1, a_2 \in A$. The agent with characteristic a_1 plays against an agent with characteristic a_2, and the transition rate to have $(m-1)$ new agents with characteristic a_1 after this game is given by

$$J_m(a_1,h\delta_{\mathbf{a}}) - J_m(a_2,h\delta_{\mathbf{a}}), \tag{132}$$

where

(i) $h\delta_{\mathbf{a}}$ is a positive measure on A described by (123), and $h > 0$ is the scale or the genetic relevance of each individual;

(ii) the definition of $J_m : \mathbb{M}^+(A) \times \mathbb{M}^+(A) \to \mathbb{R}$ is similar to (83), namely, $J_m(a_1, a_2) = U_m(a_1, a_2)$ for any $a_1, a_2 \in A$. The function $U_m(\cdot, \cdot)$ can be chosen arbitrarily as long as the average change equals a function $U(\cdot, \cdot)$, that is, for any $a_1, a_2 \in A$,

$$U(a_1, a_2) = \sum_{m=0}^{\infty} (m-1) U_m(a_1, a_2). \tag{133}$$

The interaction transition kernels Q_m in (125) from the generator (127)–(129) and measure $\mu \in \mathbb{M}(A)$ are of the form

$$\begin{aligned} Q_m(\mu, (a_1, a_2), db_1 \ldots db_m) = &\Big[J_m(a_1, \mu) - J_m(a_2, \mu)\Big] \delta_{a_1}(db_1) \ldots \delta_{a_1}(db_m) \\ &+ \Big[J_m(a_2, \mu) - J_m(a_1, \mu)\Big] \delta_{a_2}(db_1) \ldots \delta_{a_2}(db_m). \end{aligned} \tag{134}$$

Then

$$\begin{aligned} &\int_{A^{\sqcup}} \Big[g^+(\mathbf{b}) - g^+(a_1, a_2)\Big] Q(h\delta_{\mathbf{a}}, (a_1, a_2), d\,\mathbf{b}) \\ &\quad = \sum_{m=0}^{\infty} (m-1) \Big[g(a_1) \Big[J_m(a_1, h\delta_{\mathbf{a}}) - J_m(a_2, h\delta_{\mathbf{a}})\Big] \\ &\qquad + g(a_2) \Big[J_m(a_2, h\delta_{\mathbf{a}}) - J_m(a_1, h\delta_{\mathbf{a}})\Big]\Big] \\ &\quad = g(a_1) \Big[J(a_1, h\delta_{\mathbf{a}}) - J(a_2, h\delta_{\mathbf{a}})\Big] \\ &\qquad + g(a_2) \Big[J(a_2, h\delta_{\mathbf{a}}) - J(a_1, h\delta_{\mathbf{a}})\Big]. \end{aligned} \tag{135}$$

Therefore, if h tends to 0 and $h\delta_{\mathbf{a}}$ tends to some probability measure μ, then (by Fubini's theorem and (135)) the generator G_h in (130) has the form

$$\begin{aligned} &\frac{1}{2} \int_A \int_A g(a_1) \Big[J(a_1, \mu) - J(a_2, \mu)\Big] \mu(da_1) \mu(da_2) \\ &\qquad + \frac{1}{2} \int_A \int_A g(a_2) \Big[J(a_2, \mu) - J(a_1, \mu)\Big] \mu(da_2) \mu(da_1) \\ &\quad = \int_A \int_A g(a_1) \Big[J(a_1, \mu) - J(a_2, \mu)\Big] \mu(da_1) \mu(da_2) \\ &\quad = \int_A g(a) \Big[J(a, \mu) - J(\mu, \mu)\Big] \mu(da). \end{aligned}$$

Then the kinetic equation (130) has the form of the replicator dynamics in the weak topology

$$\frac{d}{dt}\int_A g(a)\mu(t,da) = \int_A g(a)\Big[J(a,\mu(t)) - J(\mu(t),\mu(t))\Big]\mu(t,da), \tag{136}$$

for $g \in \mathbb{C}(A)$.

To prove the approximation Theorem 56, we need the following concepts, where we use the notation $L^+(\mathbf{a})$ and $L^\times(\mathbf{a})$ as in Section 6.2.

(*i*) Let L be a nonnegative function in A. We say that the transition kernel is *L-subcritical* if, for all $\mathbf{b}$ in $A^\sqcup$ and μ in $\mathbb{M}^+(A)$,

$$\int_{A^\sqcup}\Big[L^+(\mathbf{b}) - L^+(a_1,a_2)\Big]Q(\mu,(a_1,a_2),d\mathbf{b}) \le 0.$$

(*ii*) We say that the transition kernel is L^+*-bounded* ($L^\times$*-bounded*) if, for all (a_1,a_2) in A^2 and μ in $\mathbb{M}^+(A)$ and some $c > 0$,

$$Q(\mu,(a_1,a_2)) \le c[L(a_1) + L(a_2)] \quad \Big(Q(\mu,(a_1,a_2)) \le cL(a_1)\cdot L(a_2)\Big).$$

(*iii*) We say that the (ND)-condition is satisfied if the number of individuals that can be created by a single act of interaction is uniformly bounded by some number m_0, and L is 1^+*-subcritical* (where 1 is a constant function).

Theorem 56 *Let A be a compact separable metric space, and let $\{U_m\}_{m=0}^\infty$ and U be bounded functions that satisfy* (133) *and*

$$\sum_{m=0}^{\infty}\int_A\int_A |m-1||U_m(a_1,a_2)|\mu(da_1)\mu(da_2) < \infty \quad \forall\mu \in \mathbb{M}^+(A). \tag{137}$$

In addition, suppose that the mapping $(\mu,\delta_{(a_1,a_2)}) \to Q(\mu,(a_1,a_2),\cdot)$ is continuous in the weak topology, where Q is defined by (126) *and* (134). *If the family of initial measures $h\delta_{\mathbf{a}}$ converges weakly to some measure μ (as $h \to 0$), then there exists a subsequence $Z_t^{h_n\delta_{\mathbf{a}}}$ of the family of stochastic process $\{Z_t^{h\delta_{\mathbf{a}}}\}_{h>0}$ defined with generator* (129) *(with transition kernel as* (126)–(134)*) that converges weakly to the solution $\mu(\cdot)$ of the replicator dynamics* (136).

Proof We will prove that the kernels Q of the generator (127)–(129) (where Q is defined by (126) and (134)) satisfy the hypotheses of theorem 4.2 in Kolokoltsov (2006).

Let $L > 0$ be an arbitrary (but fixed) positive number and μ in $\mathbb{M}(A)$. By (126), (134), and (137), we have

$$\int_{A^{\sqcup}}\left[L^{+}(\mathbf{b})-L^{+}(a_1,a_2)\right]Q(\mu,(a_1,a_2),d\,\mathbf{b})$$
$$=\sum_{m=0}^{\infty}(m-1)\Big[L\Big[J_m(a_1,\mu)-J_m(a_2,\mu)\Big]$$
$$+L\Big[J_m(a_2,\mu)-J_m(a_1,\mu)\Big]\Big]$$
$$=L\Big[J(a_1,\mu)-J(a_2,\mu)\Big]+L\Big[J(a_2,\mu)-J(a_1,\mu)\Big]=0. \tag{138}$$

and

$$Q(\mu,(a_1,a_2))=\sum_{m=0}^{\infty}\int_{A^m}Q_m(\mu,(a_1,a_2),db_1\cdots db_m)$$
$$=\sum_{m=0}^{\infty}\int_{A^m}\Big[J_m(a_1,\mu)-J_m(a_2,\mu)\Big]\delta_{a_1}(db_1)...\delta_{a_1}(db_m)$$
$$+\sum_{m=0}^{\infty}\int_{A^m}\Big[J_m(a_2,\mu)-J_m(a_1,\mu)\Big]\delta_{a_2}(db_1)...\delta_{a_2}(db_m)$$
$$=\sum_{m=0}^{\infty}m\Big[\Big[J_m(a_1,\mu)-J_m(a_2,\mu)\Big]$$
$$+\Big[J_m(a_2,\mu)-J_m(a_1,\mu)\Big]\Big]=0. \tag{139}$$

Then by (138) the kernel $Q(\mu,(a_1,a_2),d\mathbf{b})$ is L-subcritical and 1-sub-critical. By (139) the transition kernel is $(1+L^{\alpha})^{+}$-bounded. The (ND) condition is satisfied since the number of individuals that can be created by a single act of interaction is equal to 0. Thus the hypotheses of theorem 4.2 in Kolokoltsov (2006) are satisfied and the assertion follows. □

Remark 57 *Under the conditions of Theorem 56, and since the payoff function U is bounded, from Proposition 11 and Theorem 24 the replicator dynamics in weak form* (136) *equal the strong form* (85). *Therefore, there exists a subsequence* $Z_t^{h_n\delta_a}$ *of the family of stochastic process* $\{Z_t^{h\delta_a}\}_{h>0}$ *defined with generator* (126)–(129) *(with transition kernel as in* (126)–(134)*) that converges weakly to the solution* $\mu(\cdot)$ *of the replicator dynamics in the strong form* (85).

6.4 Comments

In this section we considered the replicator dynamics as a limit of a sequence of measure-valued Markov processes. We used a technique proposed by Kolokoltsov (2006, 2010) to approximate a sequence of pure-jump models of binary interaction (in the space of measures) by means of a deterministic dynamical system.

There are many questions, however, that remain open. For instance, can we have numerical approximations for these measure-valued Markov processes? This is an important issue for the application of this theory. When the set of pure strategies is finite, there are other evolutionary dynamics that can be seen as a limit of a sequence of measure-valued Markov processes. Is this true for games with strategies in a space of measures? And finally, can the replicator dynamics in the asymmetric case also be approximated by a sequence of stochastic processes?

On the other hand, some phenomena of evolutionary economics naturally intersect with a stochastic systems approach (see Dosi and Nelson (1994)). Some evolutionary dynamics can serve as an approach to understanding economic systems, even within stochastic environments that are characterized by variability and uncertainty; see for instance Safarzyńska and van den Bergh (2010). These stochastic environments include

(*i*) the evolution of industrial innovations and business strategies in markets with uncertain conditions;
(*ii*) evolutionary models where variables such as prices, product demand, market information, and the value of financial assets fluctuate in random environments.

Therefore, the theory of evolutionary economics and stochastic systems often intertwines in studies focused on the evolution and adaptation of firms in markets within economic environments marked by variability and uncertainty; see for instance Winter et al. (2003).

7 Conclusions and Suggestions for Future Research

This Element provides a general framework to study the replicator dynamics for evolutionary games in which the strategy set is a separable metric space. We analyzed the asymmetric and symmetric cases and included examples to illustrate our results.

For games in the asymmetric case we concluded the following:

(*i*) Under some conditions, there exists the solution for the asymmetric replicator equations (Theorem 12) and this solution has special characteristics (Theorem 13). In particular, these conditions are satisfied when the payoffs are bounded (Proposition 11).
(*ii*) If $\mu^* = (\mu_1^*, \ldots, \mu_n^*)$ is a Nash equilibrium of a normal-form game Γ, then μ^* is a critical point of the replicator dynamics (Theorem 16).

(*iii*) A strong uninvadable profile (SUP) is a Nash equilibrium (Theorem 19). The SUPs are Nash equilibria where the strategy of each player is dominant in a certain subset of their strategy set.

(*iv*) If μ^* is a pure Nash equilibrium and is also a SUP, then μ^* is a stable point for the replicator dynamics (Proposition 11).

(*v*) The symmetric replicator dynamics can be deduced from the asymmetric case (see Section 3.2.1). Therefore, parts (*i*) to (*iv*) are true for the symmetric case.

(*vi*) Finally, for asymmetric games, our framework provides us with robust solutions to such outstanding issues as oligopoly pricing from an evolutionary perspective. We gave three examples: the first one may be applicable to oligopoly models, theory of international trade, and public good models; the second and third examples deal with the tragedy of commons game and a model of poverty traps.

In a two-player normal-form game Γ a symmetric Nash equilibrium can be expressed in terms of a strategy called a Nash equilibrium strategy (NES). In the same form, a symmetric SUP can be written in terms of a strategy called a *strongly uninvadable strategy* (SUS). This particular fact allows us to obtain more stability results than in the asymmetric case. In our case, the replicator dynamics evolve in a space of signed measures. This allows us to study stability criteria for the replicator dynamics with respect to different topologies and metrics on a space of probability measures.

The conclusion (*iv*) is valid for a pure NES and in terms of the total variation norm $\|\cdot\|$. Let r be any metric on the set $\mathbb{P}(A)$ of probability measures, and let r-SUS be a SUS in terms of r (see Definition 26). This is a important point: a SUS is a strategy with dominance in a certain subset of the strategy set. The "size" of the subset is determined by the metric r.

For games in the symmetric case we concluded the following:

(*vii*) For any metric r, if μ^* is a r-SUS, then μ is a NES (Proposition 29).

(*viii*) If μ^* is a stable point for the replicator dynamics, then μ^* is a NES (Proposition 4.14).

(*ix*) For any metric r, if μ^* is a r-SUS, then μ^* is a stable point for the replicator dynamics (Theorems 31, 32, 33).

(*x*) Let $\mathcal{C}$ and $\mathcal{S}$ be the sets of critical and stable points of the replicator dynamics, respectively. Let $\mathcal{N}$ be the set of NESs and r-$\mathcal{SUS}$ the set of SUSs. Then we have the following relations (Theorem 38):

$$r\text{-}\mathcal{SUS} \subset \mathcal{S} \subset \mathcal{N} \subset \mathcal{C}.$$

(xi) We also analyzed the implications between the different concepts of stability in diagram (100).

(xii) The replicator dynamics in a space of measures can be approximated by a sequence of finite-dimensional dynamical systems (Theorems 43, 50.)

($xiii$) The replicator dynamics in a space of measure can be approximated by a sequence of measure-valued Markov processes (Theorem 56.)

Our proposed framework for the replicator dynamics provides opportunities for the elaboration of new evolutionary economic models and the field of development economics. The contributions in this work pave the way for the generalization of evolutionary economic models discussed in the literature, as for instance Almudi et al. (2012), Almudi and Fatas-Villafranca (2021), and Safarzyńska and van den Bergh (2010). Similarly for evolutionary macroeconomic models, some of which involve replicator mechanisms, recently analyzed through simulations (e.g. see Dosi et al. (2010) or Almudi et al. (2020b)).

Future research could explore the application of replicator dynamics in Banach spaces to extend Lotka–Volterra-type models in evolutionary economics, such as Richard Goodwin's model (Goodwin, 1967), which analyze unemployment, profit, and wage growth, where additionally, it would be valuable to complement this analysis with a dynamic income distribution component.

For future research related to evolutionary games we have several questions in mind, mainly related to the asymmetric case.

(a) In symmetric evolutionary games with strategies in the space of measures, there are stability conditions with different metrics and topologies. Are these conditions satisfied in the asymmetric case?

(b) It would be interesting to investigate if the replicator dynamics with continuous strategies in the asymmetric case can be approximated, in some sense, by games with discrete strategies. (This is true for the symmetric case; see Section 4.7.)

(c) Sandholm (2001) establishes an important relation between potential games and evolutionary dynamics for games with finite strategy sets. Under some conditions, the potential of a normal-form game is a Lyapunov function for the evolutionary dynamics. Cheung (2014) extends these results to symmetric games with strategies in a space of measures. Are these results true for the asymmetric case?

(d) For normal-form games with finite strategy sets, with the replicator dynamics we can give a geometric characterization of the set of Nash equilibria;

see Harsanyi (1973), Hofbauer and Sigmund (1998), Ritzberger (1994). Is this geometric characterization true for games with strategies in a space of measures?

(*e*) When the set of pure strategies is finite, Cressman (1997) shows that under some conditions the stability of monotone selection dynamics is locally determined by the replicator dynamics. Is this true for games with strategies on the space $\mathbb{P}(A)$ of probability measures?

(*f*) Another important issue would be to obtain a stability theorem for several evolutionary dynamics of games with continuous strategies and analyze their relation with the replicator dynamics. See Hofbauer and Sigmund (2003) (theorem 14) for games with a finite strategy set A.

(*g*) We considered the replicator dynamics as a limit of a sequence of measure-valued Markov processes. Can we obtain numerical approximations for these measure-valued Markov processes? This is an important issue for the application of the theory.

(*h*) When the set of pure strategies is finite, there are several evolutionary dynamics that can be seen as a limit of a sequence of measure-valued Markov processes. Is this true for games with strategies in a space of measures? Finally, can the replicator dynamics in the asymmetric case be approximated by a sequence of stochastic processes?

Symbols and Abbreviations

Symbols

Symbol	Description
$\mathcal{B}(A)$	Borel σ-algebra of a metric space A, p. 5
$\mathbb{M}(A)$	space of signed measure on $\mathcal{B}(A)$, p. 5
$(\mathbb{M}(A), \|\cdot\|)$	the space $\mathbb{M}(A)$ endowed with the total variation norm (1), p. 5
$\mathbb{B}(A)$	space of real-valued bounded functions on A, endowed with the supremum norm (2), p. 5
$\mathbb{C}_B(A)$	space of real-valued continuous and bounded functions on A. p. 5
$\langle \cdot, \cdot \rangle$	the dual relation (3), p. 5
$\mathcal{V}_\epsilon^{\mathcal{H}}(\mu)$	neighborhood (4) of the weak topology in $\mathbb{M}(A)$, p. 6
$\mathbb{P}(A)$	space of probability measures on $\mathcal{B}(A)$, pp. 6, 6
r_p	Prokhorov metric (6), p. 6
r_{bl}	bounded Lipschitz metric (7), p. 6
$\mathbb{L}(A)$	subspace of $\mathbb{C}_B(A)$ defined in p. 7
$\|\cdot\|_L$	norm (8) of the space $\mathbb{L}(A)$, p. 6
$\mathbb{L}_B(A)$	subspace of $\mathbb{C}_B(A)$ defined in p. 6
$\|\cdot\|_{BL}$	norm (9) of the space $\mathbb{L}_B(A)$, p. 7
r_{kr}	Kantorovich–Rubinstein metric (10), p. 7
r_{w_p}	L^p- Wasserstein distance (12), p. 7
r_w	L^1- Wasserstein distance (12), p. 7
r_{w^*}	any metric that metrizes the weak topology in $\mathbb{P}(A)$; see Remark 2, p. 8
r	any metric on $\mathbb{P}(A)$; see Remark 2, p. 8
$\mathcal{V}_\alpha^r(\mu)$	open ball (13) in the metric space $(\mathbb{P}(A), r)$, p. 8
$\mu'(t)$	strong derivative of $\mu(t)$ w.r.t. t (see Definition 5), p. 9. In Section 5.3, $\mu'(t)$ refers to the weak derivative; see Remark 47, p. 59
$J_i(\cdot)$	payoff function (18) of player i, p. 10
$\mathcal{I}_{(\mu_1,\ldots,\mu_n)}U_i$	integral operator (20)–(21), p. 11
Γ	normal-form game (23), p. 11
Γ_s	two-player normal-form game (24), p. 11

$J(\cdot)$	payoff function (18), (85) for Γ_s, pp. 11, 38
$\mathcal{N}$	set of NESs of Γ_s, p. 42
$\mathcal{C}$	set of critical points of (87), p. 42
$r - \mathcal{SUS}$	set of r-SUSs, p. 42
$K(\cdot,\cdot)$	Kullback–Leibler distance (96), p. 43
$\mathcal{W}_{\varphi(\epsilon)}(\mu)$	set defined in (94), p. 43
$[r_1,r_2]$-S	$[r_1,r_2]$-stable p. 47
$[r_1,r_2] - \mathcal{S}$	set of $[r_1,r_2]$-S points p. 49
$\mathbb{C}_\infty(A)$	space of real-valued continuous functions vanishing at infinity, p. 69
A^j	Cartesian product $A \times \cdots \times A$ (j-times), p. 70
A^∞	Cartesian product $A \times A \times \cdots$, p. 70
$A^\sqcup$	disjoint union of the Cartesian products A^j, p. 70

Abbreviations

Abbreviation	**Description**
NES	Nash equilibrium strategy, p. 12
SUP	strong uninvadable profile, p. 30
r-SUS	r-strongly uninvadable strategy, p. 41

References

Accinelli, E., and E. J. Sánchez Carrera. The evolutionary game of poverty traps. *The Manchester School*, 80(4):381–400, 2012.

Almudi, I., and F. Fatas-Villafranca. *Coevolution in economic systems*. Cambridge University Press, Cambridge, 2021.

Almudi, I., F. Fatas-Villafranca, C. M. Fernandez-Marquez, J. Potts, and F. J. Vazquez. Absorptive capacity in a two-sector neo-Schumpeterian model: A new role for innovation policy. *Industrial and Corporate Change*, 29(2):507–531, 2020a.

Almudi, I., F. Fatas-Villafranca, and L. R. Izquierdo. Innovation, catch-up, and leadership in science-based industries. *Industrial and Corporate Change*, 21(2):345–375, 2012.

Almudi, I., F. Fatas-Villafranca, G. Jarne, and J. Sanchez-Choliz. An evolutionary growth model with banking activity. *Metroeconomica*, 71(2):392–430, 2020b.

Almudi, I., F. Fatas-Villafranca, J. Palacio, and J. Sanchez-Choliz. Pricing routines and industrial dynamics. *Journal of Evolutionary Economics*, 30(3):705–739, 2020c.

Amir, R., I. V. Evstigneev, T. Hens, and L. Xu. Evolutionary finance and dynamic games. *Mathematics and Financial Economics*, 5(3):161–184, 2011.

Amir, R., I. V. Evstigneev, and K. R. Schenk-Hoppé. Asset market games of survival: A synthesis of evolutionary and dynamic games. *Annals of Finance*, 9(2):121–144, 2013.

Araujo, R. A. An evolutionary game theory approach to combat money laundering. *Journal of Money Laundering Control*, 13(1):70, 2010.

Araujo, R. A., and N. A. de Souza. An evolutionary game theory approach to the dynamics of the labour market: A formal and informal perspective. *Structural Change and Economic Dynamics*, 21(2):101–110, 2010.

Axelrod, R., and W. D. Hamilton. The evolution of cooperation. *Science*, 211(4489):1390–1396, 1981.

Balkenborg, D., and K. H. Schlag. On the evolutionary selection of sets of Nash equilibria. *Journal of Economic Theory*, 133(1):295–315, 2007.

Barelli, P., and I. Meneghel. A note on the equilibrium existence problem in discontinuous games. *Econometrica*, 81(2):813–824, 2013.

Bartle, R. G. *The elements of integration and Lebesgue measure*. John Wiley & Sons, New York, 1995.

Bauch, C. T. Imitation dynamics predict vaccinating behaviour. *Proceedings of the Royal Society of London B: Biological Sciences*, 272(1573):1669–1675, 2005.

Benaim, M., and J. W. Weibull. Deterministic approximation of stochastic evolution in games. *Econometrica*, 71(3):873–903, 2003.

Billingsley, P. *Convergence of probability measures*. John Wiley & Sons, New York, 2013.

Bischi, G. I., F. Lamantia, and D. Radi. An evolutionary Cournot model with limited market knowledge. *Journal of Economic Behavior & Organization*, 116(C):219–238, 2015.

Bishop, D., and C. Cannings. A generalized war of attrition. *Journal of Theoretical Biology*, 70(1):85–124, 1978.

Bobrowski, A. *Functional analysis for probability and stochastic processes: An introduction*. Cambridge University Press, Cambridge, 2005.

Bogachev, V. I. *Measure theory*, volume 2. Springer, Berlin, 2007.

Bomze, I. M. Dynamical aspects of evolutionary stability. *Monatshefte für Mathematik*, 110(3–4):189–206, 1990.

Bomze, I. M. Cross entropy minimization in uninvadable states of complex populations. *Journal of Mathematical Biology*, 30(1):73–87, 1991.

Bomze, I. M., and B. M. Pötscher. *Game theoretical foundations of evolutionary stability*. Lecture Notes in Economics and Mathematical Systems, 324, Springer, Berlin, 1989.

Böttcher, B., R. Schilling, and J. Wang. *Lévy matters III: Lévy-type processes: Construction, approximation and sample path properties*. Lecture Notes in Mathematics, 2099. Springer, Cham, 2013.

Carbonell-Nicolau, O. On the existence of pure-strategy perfect equilibrium in discontinuous games. *Games and Economic Behavior*, 71(1):23–48, 2011.

Carmona, G. An existence result for discontinuous games. *Journal of Economic Theory*, 144(3):1333–1340, 2009.

Carmona, G., and K. Podczeck. Existence of Nash equilibrium in games with a measure space of players and discontinuous payoff functions. *Journal of Economic Theory*, 152(1):130–178, 2014.

Cheung, M.-W. Pairwise comparison dynamics for games with continuous strategy space. *Journal of Economic Theory*, 153(1):344–375, 2014.

Cheung, M.-W. Imitative dynamics for games with continuous strategy space. *Games and Economic Behavior*, 99(C):206–223, 2016.

Cleveland, J., and A. S. Ackleh. Evolutionary game theory on measure spaces: Well-posedness. *Nonlinear Analysis: Real World Applications*, 14(1):785–797, 2013.

Corradi, V. and R. Sarin. Continuous approximations of stochastic evolutionary game dynamics. *Journal of Economic Theory*, 94(2):163–191, 2000. Corrigendum: *Journal of Economic Theory*, 140(1) (2008).

Cressman, R. Local stability of smooth selection dynamics for normal form games. *Mathematical Social Sciences*, 34(1):1–19, 1997.

Cressman, R. *Evolutionary dynamics and extensive form games*, volume 5. Massachusetts Institute of Technology Press, London, 2003.

Cressman, R. Stability of the replicator equation with continuous strategy space. *Mathematical Social Sciences*, 50(2):127–147, 2005.

Cressman, R. Continuously stable strategies, neighborhood superiority and two-player games with continuous strategy space. *International Journal of Game Theory*, 38(2):221–247, 2009.

Cressman, R., and J. Hofbauer. Measure dynamics on a one-dimensional continuous trait space: Theoretical foundations for adaptive dynamics. *Theoretical Population Biology*, 67(1):47–59, 2005.

Cressman, R., J. Hofbauer, and F. Riedel. Stability of the replicator equation for a single species with a multi-dimensional continuous trait space. *Journal of Theoretical Biology*, 239(2):273–288, 2006.

Cressman, R., W. G. Morrison, and J.-F. Wen. On the evolutionary dynamics of crime. *Canadian Journal of Economics*, 31(5):1101–1117, 1998.

Dasgupta, P., and E. Maskin. The existence of equilibrium in discontinuous economic games, I: Theory. *The Review of Economic Studies*, 53(1):1–26, 1986a.

Dasgupta, P., and E. Maskin. The existence of equilibrium in discontinuous economic games, II: Applications. *The Review of Economic Studies*, 53(1):27–41, 1986b.

Dosi, G., and R. R. Nelson. An introduction to evolutionary theories in economics. *Journal of Evolutionary Economics*, 4(3):153–172, 1994.

Dosi, G., G. Fagiolo, and A. Roventini. Schumpeter meeting Keynes: A policy-friendly model of endogenous growth and business cycles. *Journal of Economic Dynamics and Control*, 34(9):1748–1767, 2010.

Dynkin, E. B. *An introduction to branching measure-valued processes*. American Mathematical Society, Providence (Rhode Island), 1994.

Eshel, I. and E. Sansone. Evolutionary and dynamic stability in continuous population games. *Journal of Mathematical Biology*, 46(5):445–459, 2003.

Ethier, S. N., and T. G. Kurtz. *Markov processes: Characterization and convergence*, volume 282. John Wiley & Sons, New York, 1984.

Fudenberg, D., and J. Tirole. *Game theory, 1991*. Massachusetts Institute of Technology Press, Cambridge, 1991.

Fujita, M., P. R. Krugman, and A. J. Venables. *The spatial economy: Cities, regions, and international trade*. Massachusetts Institute of Technology Press, London, 2001.

Gatenby, R. A., and R. J. Gillies. A microenvironmental model of carcinogenesis. *Nature Reviews Cancer*, 8(1):56–61, 2008.

Gibbons, R. *Game theory for applied economists*. Princeton University Press, Princeton, 1992.

Givens, C. R., and R. M. Shortt. A class of Wasserstein metrics for probability distributions. *The Michigan Mathematical Journal*, 31(2):231–240, 1984.

Glicksberg, I. L. A further generalization of the Kakutani fixed point theorem, with application to Nash equilibrium points. *Proceedings of the American Mathematical Society*, 3(1):170–174, 1952.

Goodwin, R. M. A growth cycle. In C. Feinstein, editor, *Socialism Capitalism and Economic Growth*, pages 165–170. Cambridge University Press, Cambridge, 1967.

Harsanyi, J. C. Oddness of the number of equilibrium points: A new proof. *International Journal of Game Theory*, 2(1):235–250, 1973.

Heidergott, B. and H. Leahu. Weak differentiability of product measures. *Mathematics of Operations Research*, 35(1):27–51, 2010.

Heifetz, A., C. Shannon, and Y. Spiegel. The dynamic evolution of preferences. *Economic Theory*, 32(2):251–286, 2007.

Hewitt, E., and L. J. Savage. Symmetric measures on Cartesian products. *Transactions of the American Mathematical Society*, 80(2):470–501, 1955.

Hofbauer, J., and K. Sigmund. *Evolutionary games and population dynamics*. Cambridge University Press, Cambridge, 1998.

Hofbauer, J., and K. Sigmund. Evolutionary game dynamics. *Bulletin of the American Mathematical Society*, 40(4):479–519, 2003.

Hofbauer, J., and J. W. Weibull. Evolutionary selection against dominated strategies. *Journal of Economic Theory*, 71(2):558–573, 1996.

Hofbauer, J., J. Oechssler, and F. Riedel. Brown–von Neumann–Nash dynamics: The continuous strategy case. *Games and Economic Behavior*, 65(2):406–429, 2009.

Hummert, S., K. Bohl, D. Basanta et al. Evolutionary game theory: Cells as players. *Molecular BioSystems*, 10(12):3044–3065, 2014.

Kallenberg, O. *Foundations of modern probability*. Springer, New York, 2002.

Katsikas, S., V. Kolokoltsov, and W. Yang. Evolutionary inspection and corruption games. *Games*, 7(4):31, 2016.

Kolokoltsov, V. N. Kinetic equations for the pure jump models of k-nary interacting particle systems. *Markov Process and Related Fields*, 12(1):95–138, 2006.

Kolokoltsov, V. N. *Nonlinear Markov processes and kinetic equations*, volume 182. Cambridge University Press, Cambridge, 2010.

Kolokoltsov, V. N. and O. A. Malafeyev. *Understanding game theory: Introduction to the analysis of many agent systems with competition and cooperation*. World Scientific, Singapore, 2010.

Kou, P., Y. Han, and Y. Li. An evolutionary analysis of corruption in the process of collecting environmental tax in China. *Environmental Science and Pollution Research*, 28(39):54852–54862, 2021.

Kravvaritis, D., and V. G. Papanicolaou. Singular equilibrium solutions for a replicator dynamics model. *Electronic Journal of Differential Equations*, 2011(87):1–8, 2011.

Kravvaritis, D., V. G. Papanicolaou, and A. N. Yannacopoulos. Similarity solutions for a replicator dynamics equation. *Indiana University Mathematics Journal*, 57(4):1929–1945, 2008.

Kravvaritis, D., V. Papanicolaou, A. Xepapadeas, and A. Yannacopoulos. On a class of operator equations arising in infinite dimensional replicator dynamics. *Nonlinear Analysis: Real World Applications*, 11 (4): 2537–2556, 2010.

Kravvaritis, D., V. Papanicolaou, T. Xepapadeas, and A. Yannacopoulos. A class of infinite dimensional replicator dynamics. In *Dynamics, games and science*, volume I, pages 529–532. Springer, 2011.

Kurtz, T. G. Solutions of ordinary differential equations as limits of pure jump Markov processes. *Journal of Applied Probability*, 7(1):49–58, 1970.

Kurtz, T. G. Limit theorems for sequences of jump Markov processes approximating ordinary differential processes. *Journal of Applied Probability*, 8(2):344–356, 1971.

Lahkar, R., and F. Riedel. The logit dynamic for games with continuous strategy sets. *Games and Economic Behavior*, 2015.

Lahkar, R., S. Mukherjee, and S. Roy. Generalized perturbed best response dynamics with a continuum of strategies. *Journal of Economic Theory*, 200: 105398, 2022.

Lamantia, F. Evolutionary modelling in environmental economics. *Journal of Difference Equations and Applications*, 23(7):1255–1285, 2017.

Lang, S. *Differential and Riemannian manifolds*. Springer-Verlag, New York, 1995.

Lewontin, R. C. Evolution and the theory of games. *Journal of Theoretical Biology*, 1(3):382–403, 1961.

Li, Z. *Measure-valued branching Markov processes*. Springer, Berlin, 2010.

Mas-Colell, A., M. D. Whinston, and J. R. Green. *Microeconomic theory*, volume 1. Oxford University Press, New York, 1995.

Maynard Smith, J. *On evolution.* Edinburgh University Press, Edinburgh, 1972.

Maynard Smith, J. The theory of games and the evolution of animal conflicts. *Journal of Theoretical Biology*, 47(1):209–221, 1974.

Maynard Smith, J. *Evolution and the theory of games*. Cambridge University Press, Cambridge, 1982.

Maynard Smith, J., and G. A. Parker. The logic of asymmetric contests. *Animal Behaviour*, 24(1):159–175, 1976.

Maynard Smith, J., and G. R. Price. The logic of animal conflict. *Nature*, 246(5427):15–18, 1973.

McLennan, A., P. K. Monteiro, and R. Tourky. Games with discontinuous payoffs: A strengthening of Reny's existence theorem. *Econometrica*, 79(5):1643–1664, 2011.

Mendoza-Palacios, S., and O. Hernández-Lerma. Evolutionary dynamics on measurable strategy spaces: Asymmetric games. *Journal of Differential Equations*, 259(11):5709–5733, 2015.

Mendoza-Palacios, S., and O. Hernández-Lerma. Stability of the replicator dynamics for games in metric spaces. *Journal of Dynamics and Games*, 4(4):319–333, 2017.

Mendoza-Palacios, S., and O. Hernández-Lerma. A survey on the replicator dynamics for games with strategies in metric spaces. *Pure and Applied Functional Analysis*, 4(3):603–628, 2019.

Mendoza-Palacios, S., and O. Hernández-Lerma. The replicator dynamics for games in metric spaces: Finite approximations. In D. M. Ramsey and R. J, Renault, editors, *Advances in Dynamic Games: Annals of the International Society of Dynamic Games, vol 17*, pages 163–186. Birkhäuser, Cham, 2020.

Mendoza-Palacios, S., and A. Mercado. A note on the big push as industrialization process. In S. Mendoza-Palacios and A. Mercado, editors, *Games and evolutionary dynamics: Selected theoretical and applied developments*, pages 153–169. El Colegio de México, 2021.

Mendoza-Palacios, S., J. Berasaluce, and A. Mercado. On industrialization, human resources training, and policy coordination. *Journal of Industry, Competition and Trade*, 22(2):179–206, 2022.

Myerson, R. B. *Game theory*. Harvard University Press, London, 1997.

Narang, A., and A. Shaiju. Evolutionary stability of polymorphic profiles in asymmetric games. *Dynamic Games and Applications*, 9(4):1126–1142, 2019.

Narang, A., and A. Shaiju. Globally strong uninvadable sets of profiles in asymmetric games. *International Game Theory Review*, 22(01):1950014, 2020.

Narang, A., and A. Shaiju. Neighborhood strong superiority and evolutionary stability of polymorphic profiles in asymmetric games. *Journal of Dynamics and Games*, 9(3):253–266, 2022.

Norman, T. W. Dynamically stable sets in infinite strategy spaces. *Games and Economic Behavior*, 62(2):610–627, 2008.

Norman, T. W. Equilibrium selection and the dynamic evolution of preferences. *Games and Economic Behavior*, 74(1):311–320, 2012.

Oechssler, J., and F. Riedel. Evolutionary dynamics on infinite strategy spaces. *Economic Theory*, 17(1):141–162, 2001.

Oechssler, J., and F. Riedel. On the dynamic foundation of evolutionary stability in continuous models. *Journal of Economic Theory*, 107(2):223–252, 2002.

Osborne, M. J., and A. Rubinstein. *A course in game theory*. Massachusetts Institute of Technology Press, London, 1994.

Papanicolaou, V. G., and G. Smyrlis. Similarity solutions for a multi-dimensional replicator dynamics equation. *Nonlinear Analysis: Theory, Methods & Applications*, 71(7):3185–3196, 2009.

Parthasarathy, K. R. *Probability measures on metric spaces*. Academic Press, New York, 1967.

Pedersen, G. K. *Analysis now*. Springer, New York, 2012.

Prokopovych, P., and N. C. Yannelis. On the existence of mixed strategy Nash equilibria. *Journal of Mathematical Economics*, 52:87–97, 2014.

Quinteros, M. J., and M. J. Villena. On the dynamics and stability of the crime and punishment game. *Complexity*, 2022(3):1–14, 2022.

Rabanal, J. P. On the evolution of continuous types under replicator and gradient dynamics: Two examples. *Dynamic Games and Applications*, pages 7(1), No 6, 76–92, 2017.

Reiss, R.-D. *Approximate distributions of order statistics*. Springer, New York, 1989.

Reny, P. J. On the existence of pure and mixed strategy Nash equilibria in discontinuous games. *Econometrica*, 67(5):1029–1056, 1999.

Ritzberger, K. The theory of normal form games from the differentiable viewpoint. *International Journal of Game Theory*, 23(3):207–236, 1994.

Ritzberger, K., and J. W. Weibull. Evolutionary selection in normal-form games. *Econometrica*, 63(6):1371–1399, 1995.

Rosen, J. B. Existence and uniqueness of equilibrium points for concave *n*-person games. *Econometrica*, 33(3):520–534, 1965.

Royden, H. L. *Real analysis*. Macmillan, New York, 1988.

Ruijgrok, M. and T. W. Ruijgrok. An effective replicator equation for games with a continuous strategy set. *Dynamic Games and Applications*, 5(2): 157–179, 2015.

Safarzyńska, K., and J. C. van den Bergh. Evolutionary models in economics: A survey of methods and building blocks. *Journal of Evolutionary Economics*, 20(3):329–373, 2010.

Samuelson, L., and J. Zhang. Evolutionary stability in asymmetric games. *Journal of Economic Theory*, 57(2):363–391, 1992.

Sandholm, W. H. Potential games with continuous player sets. *Journal of Economic Theory*, 97(1):81–108, 2001.

Sandholm, W. H. Evolution and equilibrium under inexact information. *Games and Economic Behavior*, 44(2):343–378, 2003.

Sandholm, W. H. *Population games and evolutionary dynamics*. Massachusetts Institute of Technology Press, 2010.

Selten, R. A note on evolutionarily stable strategies in asymmetric animal conflicts. *Journal of Theoretical Biology*, 84(1):93–101, 1980.

Sethi, R. and E. Somanathan. The evolution of social norms in common property resource use. *The American Economic Review*, pages 766–788, 1996.

Shahi, C. and S. Kant. An evolutionary game-theoretic approach to the strategies of community members under joint forest management regime. *Forest Policy and Economics*, 9(7):763–775, 2007.

Shiryaev, A. N. *Probability*. Springer-Verlag, New York, 1996.

Simon, L. K. Games with discontinuous payoffs. *The Review of Economic Studies*, 54(4):569–597, 1987.

Van Veelen, M., and P. Spreij. Evolution in games with a continuous action space. *Economic Theory*, 39(3):355–376, 2009.

Varian, H. R. A model of sales. *The American Economic Review*, 70(4):651–659, 1980.

Varian, H. R. *Microeconomic analysis*. W. W. Norton, New York, 1992.

Villani, C. *Optimal transport: Old and new*. Springer-Verlag, Berlin, 2008.

Vincent, T. L., and R. A. Gatenby. Modeling cancer as an evolutionary game. *International Game Theory Review*, 7(03):331–346, 2005.

Webb, J. N. *Game theory: Decisions, interaction and evolution*. Springer, London, 2007.

Weibull, J. W. *Evolutionary game theory*. Massachusetts Institute of Technology Press, London, 1997.

Winter, S. G., Y. M. Kaniovski, and G. Dosi. A baseline model of industry evolution. *Journal of Evolutionary Economics*, 13(4):355–383, 2003.

Wright, S. Evolution in Mendelian populations. *Genetics*, 16(2):97, 1931.

Yang, F. and Q. Yang. Model for the spread of SIS epidemic based on evolution game. *Technology and Health Care*, 23(Suppl 1):s71–s75, 2015.

Acknowledgments

The work by Onésimo Hernández-Lerma was partially supported by Consejo Nacional de Humanidades Ciencias y Tecnologias (Conahcyt-México) grant CF-2019/263963. Moreover, the work by Saul Mendoza-Palacios was partially supported by Conahcyt-México under grant Ciencias Frontera 2019-87787.

To Edith, Paulina and Saul
SMP

To Max and Juli
OHL

Cambridge Elements

Evolutionary Economics

John Foster
University of Queensland

John Foster is Emeritus Professor of Economics and former Head of the School of Economics at the University of Queensland, Brisbane. He is Fellow of the Academy of Social Science in Australia, Life member of Clare Hall College, Cambridge and Past President of the International J. A. Schumpeter Society.

Jason Potts
RMIT University

Jason Potts is Professor of Economics at RMIT University, Melbourne. He is also an Adjunct Fellow at the Institute of Public Affairs. His research interests include technological change, economics of innovation, and economics of cities. He was the winner of the 2000 International Joseph A. Schumpeter Prize and has published over 60 articles and six books.

Isabel Almudi
University of Zaragoza

Isabel Almudi is Professor of Economics at the University of Zaragoza, Spain, where she also belongs to the Instituto de Biocomputación y Física de Sistemas Complejos. She has been Visiting Fellow at the European University Institute, Columbia University and RMIT University. Her research fields are evolutionary economics, innovation studies, environmental economics and dynamic systems.

Francisco Fatas-Villafranca
University of Zaragoza

Francisco Fatas-Villafranca is Professor of Economics at the University of Zaragoza, Spain. He has been Visiting Scholar at Columbia University and Visiting Researcher at the University of Manchester. His research focuses on economic theory and quantitative methods in the social sciences, with special interest in evolutionary economics.

David A. Harper
New York University

David A. Harper is Clinical Professor of Economics and Co-Director of the Program on the Foundations of the Market Economy at New York University. His research interests span institutional economics, Austrian economics and evolutionary economics. He has written two books and has published extensively in academic journals. He was formerly Chief Analyst and Manager at the New Zealand Treasury.

About the Series

Elements in Evolutionary Economics provides comprehensive overviews of the major building blocks of evolutionary economics across micro, meso and macro domains of analysis. It extends from theories of evolutionary economic behavior, entrepreneurship and the innovating firm, and agent-based modelling, to processes of variation and selection in evolutionary competition, industrial dynamics, evolutionary economics of institutions, emergent complexity, and evolutionary macroeconomics.

Cambridge Elements

Evolutionary Economics

Elements in the Series

A Reconsideration of the Theory of Non-Linear Scale Effects: The Sources of Varying Returns to, and Economics of, Scale
Richard G. Lipsey

Evolutionary Economics: Its Nature and Future
Geoffrey M. Hodgson

Coevolution in Economic Systems
Isabel Almudi and Francisco Fatas-Villafranca

Industrial Policy: The Coevolution of Public and Private Sources of Finance for Important Emerging and Evolving Technologies
Kenneth I. Carlaw and Richard G. Lipsey

Explaining Technology
Roger Koppl, Roberto Cazzolla Gatti, Abigail Devereaux, Brian D. Fath, James Herriot, Wim Hordijk, Stuart Kauffman, Robert E. Ulanowicz and Sergi Valverde

Evolutionary Games and the Replicator Dynamics
Saul Mendoza-Palacios and Onésimo Hernández-Lerma

A full series listing is available at: www.cambridge.org/EEVE

Printed in the United States
by Baker & Taylor Publisher Services